A Scottish Gran's Daily Dose of Wisdom

By

Catherine Sladczyk-Bew (aka Gran)

DEDICATION

This book is dedicated with love to my husband Pete, truly my "rock." The two very precious gifts in my life who call me Mum, my son Peter and daughter Lianne. Our wonderful wee grandchildren, Oliver and Sienna, who make the word "Gran" the best name in the world apart from Mum! Also, our Jay and Deniz.

In loving memory of my Mum and Dad, Catherine and Carl Sladczyk, always loved, always missed, never ever forgotten.

ACKNOWLEDGMENTS

My precious daughter Lianne, a loving presence through many lives, for her patience, laughter and support in the creation of this book.

To my gifted soul sister Susyn Blair-Hunt who inspired, encouraged and motivated me to write this book. Love you.

Kim, who shares my passion for Tarot. Michaela, Ann and Lynne for the laughter, adventures, coffee and cake we've enjoyed together over the years. Here's to more of the same!

Thank you to all those insightful authors whose words inspire and motivate. This book would not have been possible without you. I appreciate your wisdom.

January

January 1

"The Universe is so well balanced that the mere fact that you have a problem also serves as a sign that there is a solution."
~ Steve Marboli

Synchronicity in a nutshell! For example, those well-known sayings, "As above, so below," "You reap what you sew," Yin and Yang etc., sum it up perfectly. The Universe/Life is all about balance, therefore it makes sense that there is always a solution to your problem, otherwise you wouldn't know you had a problem in the first place! Know what I mean? It reminds me of that adage, "What came first, the chicken or the egg?" Darned if I know but somebody must know as there is always a solution or an answer. I just wish they would put me out of my misery and let me know...

January 2

"Do not look for sanctuary in anyone except yourself." ~ *Buddha*

In times of crisis or feeling vulnerable, it is tempting to unload our concerns onto a family member or a close friend; their understanding and advice can be invaluable. However, nobody else will ever know us as intimately as we know ourselves, therefore we also need to create within us our own place of sanctuary. Doing this will allow us to retreat to where we feel most at ease and able to view what confronts us from a place of safety. Once there, we can use the peace and tranquility of this sacred space to seek the insight and answers necessary in our battle to overcome tribulations. Only we have the power to construct our very own personal sanctuary. If you have not done so yet, now would be the time to get to work.

January 3

**"In all things of nature there is something
of the marvellous."** ~ *Aristotle*

*I love nature! The variety of flowers and plants,
colours, scents, and intricate patterns that adorn
many species of animals and winged creatures.
The fish and mammals in the oceans and rivers.
Our forests, mountains, rivers, lochs, and lakes!
So much for us to see and wonder at. None of
which has been formed or created by the hand of
man but seeded, birthed, and gifted to us by
Mother Earth. Marvellous seems a very mundane
word encompassing all that we should be grateful
for. Perhaps there are no words, other than those
from our grateful hearts, which can even come
close to expressing our gratitude for all we see in
the nature surrounding us.*

January 4

"Best rule for a simple life: Care with no reason, love with no expectations."
~ Sanjukta Mukherjee

Oh, if it were only that simple! I think that is one rule that few of us could say we are able to follow. Humans just are not made to care with no reason or love with no expectations. We always have a reason to care and have expectations of the love we give to others, and that's because we have a heart. How much simpler would life be if we followed the above and took no risks? However, consider the consequences for just a moment. Wouldn't we miss the freedom of choosing to care, of loving with the expectation that our love will be reciprocated? The reasons that make us care and love the way we do, and will always continue to, are part of who we are as human beings, without which we would only exist not live. For this, I am truly thankful.

January 5

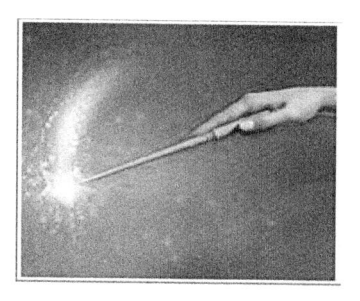

"All of your wishes can come true. It is your own doubt that blocks them from coming through." ~ *Unknown*

I guess it is easier to say "think positive" than actually act positive. However, when we make our wishes and "send them out there" do we totally believe that they are going to come true, or do we tend to think that it would be nice if they came true but how likely is that? We need to change our thinking patterns and really believe and focus on the certainty that our wishes WILL come true rather than doubt they will. Surely, it is better to be optimistic with positive expectations rather than the opposite thus allowing this positivity to enhance a possible successful outcome. Why would you do otherwise?

January 6

"People who judge, DON'T MATTER.
People who matter, DON'T JUDGE."
~ *Unknown*

This is something I have learned over the years. Occasionally, certain people are quick to judge what you do and share their, often unsolicited, unfavourable opinions with you and/or others. At first, this can seriously impact how you view who you are and what you are trying to achieve in life. However, thankfully, very quickly, most of us learn that the people who matter most to us, do not judge, only offer their support even if they have doubts about our actions. Those who judge tend to lose interest once they realise that you really do not give a fig about what they think. So there!

January 7

"Do what is right for you. No one else is walking in your shoes." ~ *Heidi Dellaire*

When I was younger, I tended to believe that everybody else knew better than me and that my opinions were worth nothing, so I tended to go along with the herd. However, along the way to reaching the age I am now, 'er ahem, my early 70s, I have reached the conclusion that, you know what, I can make meaningful decisions and hold opinions that matter. Other people's opinions are just that...opinions they have formed in their lives, not mine. Now, I am confident that my decisions and my opinions impact and reflect on my path in life, which is how it should be for each and every one of us. What do you think?

January 8

"A breakdown always leads to a breakthrough." ~ *Anna Pereira*

We have all been there, some more than others, but nobody has escaped a time or times in life when people or situations get us down so much that we find ourselves in a dark place where hope seems just a word not a possibility. However, how many times in the future have we looked back at these times and realised that we learned an important lesson which served us well later in life? Perhaps the rose-tinted spectacles at that time were discarded, either by choice or circumstance and we were able to view people, events, or situations as they actually were. If we were fortunate, we accepted what we learned, if not, we risked having to experience the same process again and again until we did. Remember, there is no place to go from downwards but upwards!

January 9

"Some people will only "love you" as much as they can use you. Their loyalty ends where the benefit stops." ~ *Surgeo Bell*

Because we are all different, it is obvious we are not all "coming from the same place." One or more people in our lives may not have our best interests at heart but use us for their own selfish needs or desires. Initially, we are happy to welcome them into our lives, but it usually does not take us too long to realise their true intent and act accordingly by leaving them by the wayside. Hopefully, if this happens to them again and again, they will learn their lesson and become better people. I have moved on from these people in the past and, no doubt, I will be doing so again in the future. Such is life!

January 10

"When you feel that something is a sign from Heaven.... trust that feeling."
~ Unknown

Ooo, don't you just love it when that happens? That feeling you get, the assurance that there is a message just for you from Spirit, The Angels, a Higher Power. There is no reason for you to know something, but you just do, you "feel" it in your very soul, your very being. No explanation needed. You have got the message and how special is that? I personally believe we usually get a "message" or a "sign" because of troubles or trials we are experiencing in our lives at any given time so isn't it wonderful to know that we are being looked on and after by such a powerful, healing, loving, benevolent Spirit? I, for one, completely trust and treasure these signs.

January 11

"Don't do something permanently stupid because you are temporarily upset."
~ Zig Ziglar

I can so relate to this, and I expect many of you can also? It is human instinct to retaliate in anger when we feel threatened or attacked via social media in these days of the internet and global messaging. The impulse to dash off an angry response, perhaps saying things we shouldn't, and click it into being before we've given ourselves time to consider the potential repercussions consumes us! Indeed, we may feel smug and very pleased with ourselves for, in our opinion, our brilliant and cutting choice of words in return. However, there is no taking back what has been delivered to their inbox. Not easy I know, but in situations like this why not step away from your pc, have a cuppa, go for a walk, or distract yourself in some way? Anything to give you time and space to consider what has been said before you respond. Then, think about the impact of your

reply on your conscience and the recipient before placing your fingers on the keyboard.

January 12

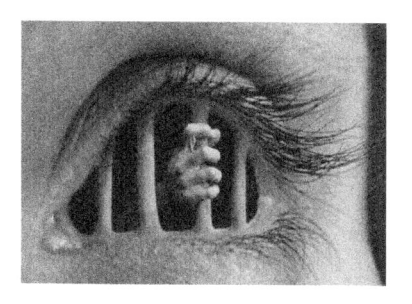

"The greatest prison that people live in is the fear of what other people think."
~ David Icke

Not caring what everybody else thinks about us is not an easy achievement. In fact, we go through life adhering to rules and regulations (well, most of us do), so we let the world know we are complying and conforming and being "good." However, regarding our family, friends, work colleagues, etc., we can be guilty of conforming to their ideas of how we should behave and think. So much so that we stifle the very things that make us whom we are therefore denying ourselves the opportunity of thinking and behaving "outside the box." Why should we care what other people think of us? Would it really affect us that much? Would stifling our creativity and individuality add anything to their lives? Of course not! Always be true to yourself on your life path and take pleasure in being who you are not other peoples' idea of who you should be.

January 13

"As you walk upon the sacred earth, treat each step as a prayer." ~ *Black Elk*

These days our poor planet is certainly being repeatedly abused and disrespected. Whether it be war causing chaos and destruction, the abuse of our forests, the killing of our wildlife, or the effects of global warming, it does not paint us in a good light, does it? We who inhabit this beautiful planet need to realise that this is the only world we have. Therefore, we should be thankful, treasure and protect what we have. We need to respect our good earth for the blessings it provides in food, water, shelter, and our flora and fauna. As individuals, we each have the opportunity to do our personal best every single day in respecting and nurturing what surrounds us in recognition of the gifts we have been granted by our beautiful, unique planet Earth. Each time we do, I believe a prayer is generated asking that our wonderful world grows, prospers, and flourishes for the generations who will follow.

January 14

"An early morning walk is a blessing for the whole day." ~ *Henry David Thoreau*

The best time of day to take the opportunity to enjoy and commune with whatever Higher Being you believe in is during an early morning walk. "You time" before the day gets hijacked by commitments, work, school runs, chores, errands etc. Get your fill of the peace and quiet, stillness, and tranquility, in creating a clear head and peaceful spirit, which will stand you in good stead for the rest of the day. Most importantly of all, just feel blessed for being alive and able to enjoy the beginning of a new day in your life when anything and everything is possible.

January 15

"Learning to be alone, and enjoying it, is the most empowering gift you can give yourself." ~ *Steven Aitchison*

I am very much a people person and enjoy the company of my family and friends and appreciate meeting new people and getting to know them. However, I also treasure time spent on my own and am never at a loss as to how to occupy myself. Just to take me away from the hurly-burly of everyday life for a while to enjoy my own company and, more often than not, to take the opportunity to discover and explore more about what interests me personally, what gives me pleasure, and what enhances my Spiritual knowledge. I believe this not only benefits me but those who know me as my increased Spiritual awareness is often shared with them for their benefit.

January 16

"You may not end up where you thought you'd be, but you always end up where you're meant to be." ~ *Unknown*

Many of us will be surprised and perhaps even shocked by where we find ourselves at different times in our lives but, think about it, is it so unexpected? We all have our goals, expectations, and dreams on which to focus and work toward achieving. We form pictures in our minds of our expectations, but unfortunately, it does not always work out the way we imagined or planned. Situations, people, and obstacles, over which we have no control, can often impact, and knock us off course onto a hitherto unknown path and this affects where and when we will ultimately finish up. If you believe that everything happens for a reason, as I do, then you will realise that, ultimately, you might not end up where you had in mind, but that you will always end up exactly where you were meant to be, and it is best just to be accepting and compliant.

January 17

"Be mindful of your self-talk. It's a conversation with the Universe."
~ *David James Lees*

Most people I know believe that the Universe hears and acknowledges everything we put "out there" and does, in fact, respond. As an example, send out a positive thought and you will receive a positive response. Alternatively, send out a negative thought and you will receive a negative response. I think that makes perfect sense, don't you? Therefore, being the sensible and intelligent beings we are, we should be extremely mindful of what we say when we converse with ourselves as everything we say will be heard, acted upon, and responded to in kind. Surely too, it is sensible to "transmit" from a positive and optimistic frame of mind as this gives us the added benefit of helping guide the Universe to our specific coordinates. Self-doubt needs to be relegated to a faraway galaxy! May the Force be with you!

January 18

"On particularly rough days when I'm sure I can't possibly endure, I like to remind myself that my track record for getting through rough days so far is 100%.... and that's pretty good." ~ *Unknown*

"Pretty good? I would say it was fantastic! We can all relate to this can't we? I know I can. What is the alternative when life strews your path with pain either physical or mental, sorrow, self-doubt, debt, or anything that has the power to torment and torture us? This could be the last straw in an increasing list of disasters to target us and our feelings of frustration and anger may threaten to overwhelm us. However, here's the thing to keep in mind, you have been here before, perhaps more times than you'd like to remember, and everything got resolved, didn't it? You coped, moved on, and put it behind you, didn't you? So, what's so different this time? Exactly...nothing! Know and believe that it is going to be ok this time too and it will, you'll see!

January 19

"A negative mind will <u>never</u> give you a positive life." ~ *Ziad K. Abdelnour*

How could it? If your mind is filled with negative thoughts that prevent you from following your dreams, applying for that brilliant job opportunity, striking up a conversation with someone you want to get to know, etc., who do you think is to blame? You, of course! Once you have established a negative thought pattern the only person who can take action to change it to a positive is you so what are you waiting for? Flick your "switch" to positive and see how the world responds. Positive attracts positive so think positively for long enough and it will become your mindset so there will be no stopping you then. Look out world!

January 20

"If you're spending a lot of time working on your relationship, then the relationship is not working." ~ *Marshall Van Summers*

Although I believe that, to create a harmonious, fulfilling, loving relationship, the two people involved do have to work at it, there is a difference between working and "working." A good relationship means working together, being in harmony (most of the time), and being of one mind in building and sustaining the feelings between you. If you feel you are getting no support, your affection is not being returned, you are being ignored, or that the relationship has, in fact, become hard work, that is the time to assess your relationship.

January 21

"May you live every day of your life."
~ Jonathan Swift

What a lovely wish and profound few words. Sometimes, many of us are so busy dealing with the everyday needs and demands our busy lives make on us, that we forget to just "live!" By this, I mean being aware and realising just how very precious life is and that every second, minute, hour, and day that passes has gone forever. So, slow down a little, try to live in the moment more and appreciate the blessings you have instead of whinging about what you think you should have but don't. Basically, live a life surrounded by those you love most and make sure it's full of love, laughter, adventures, new beginnings and, dreams...Off you go!

January 22

"You are not responsible for other peoples' happiness. When making decisions put your own happiness first."
~ Steven Aitchison

Well, I agree with this up to a point but then again, what makes each of us happy varies from person to person. I'm happy if those I love and care about in my life are healthy and contented; if my days are productive in what I love to do and ecstatic if I get my hands on my favourite chocolates! Obviously, be aware of how your decisions will affect those closest to you but, ultimately, the people we interact most with are solely responsible for their perception of what or who manifests happiness for them, just as you are. So, make your decisions based on creating your own happiness, which is something we are all capable of doing. If you don't put yourself first, then who will? We all have a checklist of what makes us happy and what works for one may not work for all.

January 23

"Some of us think holding on makes us strong; but sometimes it's letting go."
~ *Hermann Hesse*

Occasionally, people in our lives are only meant to be with us for a certain length of time before, for whatever reason, they wish to move on. However, if we are not ready to let them go when they want to, "Houston we have a problem!" Being weak is refusing to accept that they don't want to share their life with us any longer. Pleading with them to stay may, on occasion, cause them to feel sorry for us, relent and agree to give the relationship another go. However, if their heart isn't in it and your relationship is still not what it should be, then perhaps it's time to be strong in letting them go. You are not being strong by hanging on if it is not meant to be, only deluding yourself. Letting go is not being weak it is being realistic and therefore being strong in taking the best course of action for them and, more importantly, for you.

January 24

"Do not go where the path may lead, go instead where there is no path and leave a trail." ~ *Ralph Waldo Emerson*

Sounds exciting but a wee bit scary, doesn't it? Ignore a nice safe path, take a leap of faith, and step off into the unknown, eek! However, how much more exciting would it be if we were brave enough to do just that and forge our very own unique pathway to a potentially adventurous new destination? In doing so, having the opportunity to lay, one by one, the steppingstones of our innovative ideas, discoveries, challenges, and triumphs for others to follow. This acknowledges and pays tribute to those who came before who were brave and determined in creating a path for future generations to benefit from in retracing their steps. No mean task but the rewards in doing so may mean more to you personally than you could ever imagine, not least in progressing on your journey to Spirituality.

January 25

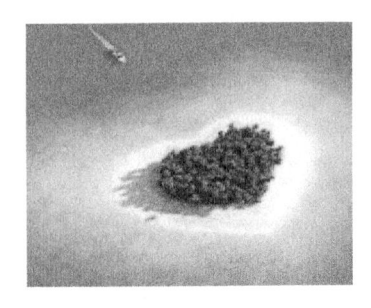

"Remember that, wherever your heart is, there you will find your treasure."
~ Paulo Coelho

Sometimes we are so caught up in just coping with life that we lose sight of what is important to us, i.e., our family and friends. Our endeavours in earning money, acquiring "stuff," and time spent doing things we enjoy, can divert our attention away from those who love and want to spend time with us. It's often too easy to unintentionally neglect our nearest and dearest just by being thoughtless, not heartless. So, ensure you always make time, whenever possible, just to show by word or deed just how deeply you love, truly value, and bless their presence in your life. Just because they live in your heart doesn't mean they don't need us to remind them now and again of why they are there!

January 26

"When something bad happens you have three choices, you can either let it define you, let it destroy you, or you can let it strengthen you." ~ *Dr. Seuss*

We do not have any control over the terrible things that happen to us all at times, but we do have a choice as to how we deal with them. We can wear it like a cloak so everyone will pity us, allow it to overcome us and bring us to our knees or deal with it and move on. I know which one I would choose, and it is neither of the former. Keeping these three choices in mind, what choice would suit you best? Yes, I thought you'd say that, so that's to your credit and your life sincerely thanks you for it!

January 27

"The earth has music for those who listen."
~ Reginald Vincent Holmes

The earth gifts us the pleasure of its own music by making use of the sounds of the creatures who inhabit the land, mountains, and waters. Listen as the breeze or wind conducts an unseen orchestra using the leaves of trees or long grass. As it whistles through the nooks and crannies of buildings. The murmurs and roars of streams and rivers as they flow over rocks searching for their ultimate end in joining a larger body. The melody of the sea ebbing and flowing on the shore or the crashing of the waves thundering against whatever seeks to defy their might. Surround yourself with any of all of these and you will truly feel at one with the earth you have been gifted to walk upon.

January 28

"Just remember you can't put your arms around a memory so <u>hug</u> someone you love today." ~ *Toni Kane*

Anybody who knows me will tell you I am a serial hugger, yes hugger, not mugger! Always have been and always will be. I am so thankful I was created this way as I have no regrets that my parents, who sadly both passed many years ago, ever suffered from a lack of hugs and kisses from me, whether they wanted them at the time or not! My children and grandchildren are also very tactile which is great, so lots of hugs and kisses there too. I wish everybody felt and behaved this way but realise that is a wish that might be stretching it a bit. Unfortunately, it makes me feel sad that I know and have known people who, at the loss of a loved one, feel full of remorse as well as grief at their loss. The reason being that they realised, too late, that they had neglected to spend enough time with them, failed to speak or show their love, could have shared more hugs with them, or simply just listened when they had

something to say. Interestingly, it has also been proved in accredited medical studies that hugs DO benefit physical health, which is not news to me personally, but hopefully gives the green light to us all in giving and receiving hugs, and more hugs, and more hugs while we can...Know what I mean? Of course, you do!

January 29

"Magic is essentially the higher understanding of nature." ~ *Unknown*

I believe we are all born with magic within us and therefore capable of manifesting and weaving our own "spells" using our intent, and this is where nature comes in. How can we not believe in magic when we behold the miracles of nature all around us every day? There is nothing quite like walking through a forest, sunlight streaming through the trees, rain making music as it kisses the leaves and ground as it falls, or crisp crunchy footfalls on a frosty day. Perhaps catching a fleeting glimpse of a beautiful forest creature or bird wary of the stranger in their midst. This is when my own belief in magic is most heightened, that something so wonderful, so Spiritually inspiring, and with no man's hand in its conception, exists for all of us to appreciate and enjoy. It inspires me to believe that I too have the ability to create and weave magic should I choose to.

January 30

**"The best feeling is when someone
appreciates everything about you that
someone else took for granted."**
~ Unknown

*This is best summed up by a very close friend of
mine who had been in a relationship with a man
who was very controlling mentally. He constantly
belittled and verbally abused her about her
weight, appearance, and behaviour. Always quick
to find fault for no reason. After almost 11 years
of his abuse, and after great emotional turmoil
and soul searching, she found the strength to
leave him. Soon after, she met a man who showed
he loved her not just by saying so, but by being
supportive, constantly praising her appearance,
appreciating everything she did for him, and by
doing whatever he could to make her happy. They
are now happily married. She has since
blossomed into the beautiful lady, inside and out,
that she was meant to. Her former partner
remains alone in life, perhaps regretting her loss.*

January 31

"An invisible thread connects those who are destined to meet, regardless of time, place, and circumstance. The thread may stretch or tangle, but it will never break."
~ Ancient Chinese Proverb

I have had too many experiences of the above to count but I am still amazed when it happens repeatedly. I expect you have all had times when you meet someone in the most unlikely place at the most inopportune moment who you just "know" was meant to come into your life, and indeed you into theirs, for a reason that may be unclear at the time. I honestly believe that, while travelling along our life path, there are certain people waiting at the side to step in beside us, whether just for a short way, a great distance or for the duration of our journey. All are important and all bring something different to share with us, some beneficial and some not so beneficial but everything has a purpose and a lesson for us, so it behooves us to just be accepting.

36

February

February 1

"Allow yourself to hope, to believe, and to trust again. Don't let a few bad memories stop you from having a good life."
~ Mandy Hale

Allowing an unhealthy relationship, friendship, or work situation to impact on us so much so that it colours our perception when experiencing them again in the future does us no favours whatsoever. It would be to our advantage to perceive this as a learning curve in realising we may just have learned a valuable lesson, albeit it a painful one. Hopefully, this realisation will prevent us from making the same mistake again in the future. It would also serve us better in our determination to be positive and optimistic in outlook rather than negative and pessimistic. Therefore, through our own negativity, prevent ourselves from living fully. Nobody knows what the future will bring but isn't it to our advantage to welcome whatever comes our way and leave past negative experiences where they belong in the past?

February 2

"No matter how you feel, get up, dress up, show up and NEVER GIVE UP!"
~ Regina Brett

We have all had those mornings when we wake up, think about the day ahead, or what went on the day before, and snuggle even further down, pulling the duvet over our head and squeezing our eyes tightly shut. It never works though, does it? You are still wide awake, aware you must get up and get on with it even though it is the last thing you want to do. The good thing is though that, usually, not always but usually, things are not as bad as we thought and being up, showered, face paint on (for us ladies and, of course, any men so inclined), dressed, and being ready to face the day is not so bad. It is this positive spirit that keeps us going and anyway, what is the alternative, ignoring life and all it has to offer, good and not so good? The need to believe that what is being offered holds potential and it is this belief that keeps us going day after day.

February 3

"I admire people who choose to shine even after all the storms they've been through."
~ Germany Kent

I really do! They inspire me to believe that I can do the same. If they can cope with all the stresses and problems that life throws at them, learn and move on, well so can I. People like this deserve our admiration for being role models for the rest of us. It is as if they are saying, look what we have been through, dealt with, overcome, and survived, so believe that you can too. Also, it helps that they have gone through a situation that we are currently experiencing and can offer comfort, reassurance and advice that there IS a light at the end of the very dark tunnel we may currently find ourselves and we just need to focus on getting there. Who has the matches?

February 4

"You must realise that fear is not real. It is a product of thoughts you create. Do not misunderstand, danger is very real, but fear is a choice." ~ *Unknown*

This reminds me of the saying that "There is nothing to fear but fear itself," which I have always thought of as very insightful and absolutely spot on. However, we all experience fear in different ways and different levels, i.e., we allow ourselves to be fearful of a situation, either imagined or real, or fear of physical harm being inflicted on us. Often, we create our own fear by our own thoughts or actions so surely, we have a choice whether to fear or not to fear? So easy to say not to fear but not so easy to avoid doing it. However, all down to personal choice, so what would you choose?

February 5

"Happy are those who take life day by day, complain very little, and are thankful for the little things in life." ~ *Faisal Dil*

I like to think this applies to me now although, like most people, it never used to. I never took the time to really "see" and appreciate the people around me or the wonders of nature. This realisation only began when I embarked on my own personal Spiritual journey, and I am so grateful that my eyes were opened to the wonders and the blessings that surround me every day. I take pleasure in time spent with my family and friends and appreciate all they bring me and take every opportunity to reciprocate their love and support. I also try, though I am not always successful, however getting there, to be thankful for all the little things that happen in my life and trying not to not be more negative than I should or is good for me.

February 6

Your life is a result of the choices you make. If you don't like your life, it is time to start making better choices."
~ Zig Ziglar

Oh, I love this one! I do so agree! This is a positive mantra for me as I totally believe that, although life can throw challenges at us that can throw us off track for a while, and construct barriers to confront us, it is up to us to jump over them, smash through them, or push them aside to confidently continue to where we want to be. Nobody else is going to offer to fix our life and why should they? We are all masters and mistresses of our own journey through life as, obviously, nobody knows us better than we do. If you want to change something, do it! Want to achieve a goal, then what's stopping you? Be POSITIVE and the sky is the limit for each and every single one of us.

February 7

"You have to love yourself because no amount of love from others is sufficient to fill the yearning that your soul requires from you." ~ *Dodinsky*

Absolutely true. If we do not love ourselves and do not value what makes and shapes us and our beliefs, then why should anybody else? To grow, not unlike a plant, we begin as a wee seed, work to root ourselves, and allow our stem to grow upwards pushing through the soil, all the while encouraged by the earth (self-love) within Continuously striving to reach the light. Our self-belief continues to nourish and encourage us, as we sprout leaves and flowers representing the people, the situations, and the choices we make, in life. This all "stemmed" from, and only became possible, by our belief in our personal potential to achieve fulfillment. Such purpose, such dedication, such strength!

February 8

"Attitude is a little thing that makes a big difference." ~ *Winston Churchill*

Attitude is wonderful, isn't it? If we have a good attitude, we are positive, ready to enjoy ourselves and cope with whatever the day presents us with, the people we encounter, the situations we find ourselves in. Like a cloak of invincibility, we wear it with confidence. However, a bad attitude on the other hand, tends to repel people, show us in a bad light, and work against us in getting what or who we want. Our attitude is what most people meeting us, perhaps for the first time, notice and react to. Much, much better to have a good attitude than the alternative, don't you think?

February 9

"Ask for what you want and be prepared to get it!" ~ *Maya Angelou*

My wonderful Scottish Grannie had a favourite saying, "If you don't ask, you don't get!" It is, and always has been, a mantra I've carried through my entire life. I am a great believer in always asking for what you want, because if you never ask, how will you know if your request will be granted? Know what I mean? Usually, when we put our request "out there" we consign it to the ether and, if nothing happens in the following five minutes, (for us impatient souls), we tend to push it to the back of our minds as day-to-day matters take over. I believe that every time we remember our wish it gives it a little push nearer to becoming reality. Try it, it works!

February 10

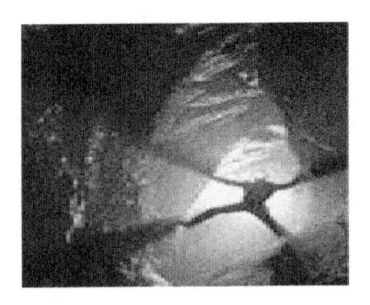

"When life puts you in tough situations don't say "Why me?" just say "Try me!"
~ Miley Cyrus

There are times when all of us are faced with demanding situations, and it's then we have two choices. We can either feel sorry for ourselves and go into total "poor me" mode, or we can "man or woman up" and think of ways to resolve whatever it is. Perhaps the tough situations presented to us are life's way of assessing us, just to see how we cope and hopefully overcome our difficulties. It would then be to our credit to adopt a brave, confident outlook and deal with them. Life, are you listening?

February 11

"Even after all this time the Sun never says to the Earth "You owe me!" Look what happens with a love like that…it lights the whole sky." ~ *Hafez*

Love should be unselfish, shouldn't it? When we love someone totally, with all our heart, our very being, we think of them and their best interests before ourselves. That's called unconditional love. In that way, we too are like the Sun because we give our love freely, willingly, without a thought for what we will get in return. It is enough for us to know that we can give so much because, in our eyes, the focus of our love is deserving of it and the ability to do this gives us joy too. Their happiness is our happiness, and this love lights up the whole sky and indeed the entire world for us and them.

February 12

"I may not be there yet, but I am closer than I was yesterday." ~ *Misty Copeland*

Sometimes our dreams and aspirations seem so distant that we may feel we will never see them realised. However, at least we have a purpose in having something to aim for which, let's face it, is better than having nothing to look forward to achieving in the future. Even if it feels as though we will never get there and perhaps, on occasion, wonder if it is worth it, remember time never stands still so every single second, minute, hour, and day that passes gets us just that bit closer to where we want to be. Never give up and remember the saying "All good things come to those who wait." That could be you!

February 13

"Everything that you are going through is preparing you for what you asked for."
~ *Unknown*

Let us say we put our wish out there to the Universe or Higher Power and believe it has been received and understood and that a process has begun in making it a reality for us. I believe that, for us to genuinely appreciate and value the result, we may have lessons to learn beforehand. Now these lessons may not be easy for us, and we may struggle to understand or comprehend what they could possibly teach us, but we need to trust that they are for our own good and will ensure that, when our wish is realised, we are in the right place mentally, physically, and spiritually to truly appreciate it.

February 14

"You are never too old to set another goal or to dream another dream." ~ *C.S. Lewis*

Of course not! Sometimes the right time to set another goal or dream another dream is when we are older and, hopefully, though not always, wiser. That is when we are free from the constraints of raising a family, working, being at other people's disposal and having no time to call our own. Enjoy and take pleasure in achieving your goals and dreams as you now have the time and freedom to do so. Never let anybody tell you that you are too old to do anything. Just make sure your health insurance is up to date and off you totter, 'er go!

February 15

"Forgiveness doesn't mean that what they did is okay. It means that you are no longer willing to carry toxic anger in your heart."
~ Doreen Virtue

All of us, at one time or another, have known betrayal by someone else. Be it in a relationship, a colleague, a family member, a friendship, whatever, despite how many times it happens it always causes us pain. It is because we believed and trusted that our betrayer had only our best interests at heart and now, we look back at our relationship with them seeking signs we may have missed that showed them for who they really were. It is extremely easy to dwell on how much they hurt us and spend time thinking of ways to retaliate by inflicting the same hurt and pain on them. However, let us forget them for a moment and think about the best way forward for us. Is it to let this hurt fester and grow unchecked within us, like a dark weight we then carry forever, or to believe, as I do, that what goes around, comes around, and that Karma, hopefully, with big jaggy teeth, has a way of

evening things up? Better to be kind to ourselves and let it go, don't you think?

February 16

"When people walk away, let them. Your future is not about people who walk away... it's about the people who stay in it for the ride" ~ *T.D. Jakes*

Sometimes when people want to walk out of our lives, we try to prevent them. Perhaps we believe they still have a part to play therefore we're reluctant to let them go. However, what if they have already played their part and it is time for them to go? Often, it's not as black and white as this for many of us at the time. Later, on looking back, we will probably only then be able to acknowledge that they actually did us a favour by leaving although we couldn't see this at the time. Look around you and appreciate the people who are still walking through life with you because that's where they're meant to be and where you're meant to be for them.

February 17

"When the dark clouds of doubt, anger or worry begin to move upon you, steady yourself in the knowledge that, in time, the storm will pass." ~ *Bryant McGill*

It is something I try to do whenever I am facing a problem, feeling angry, worrying, or occasionally when the dark cloud of just feeling low in mood seems to hover over me. I have learned, from experience, that because time passes no matter what is going on in our lives, it all eventually passes and fades into the past. So, no matter how dire things appear, I can feel reassured it is a transitory phase and I just need to focus on this fact until the "weather" forecast becomes more promising for the future.

February 18

"We do not heal the past by dwelling there; we heal the past by living fully in the present." ~ *Marianne Williamson*

Good advice, isn't it? Basically, telling us to move on and turn our energy into making the present a much better place to find ourselves living in than the past turned out to be. It is knowing when to let go and move on that we find difficult. It can be difficult to release our past to move on as everything we go through in life becomes part of us, whether we wish it to or not. We are the total sum of everything that has happened to us since we first drew breath, and which shapes us in growing into who we were meant to be. However, as we travel through life, we need to realise that, when our present has completed what it is supposed to, it then becomes our past. Therefore, we are always in motion, so our intention should be to live fully in the present not the past.

February 19

"Don't ruin a good day today by thinking about yesterday's bad day…. let it go."
~ Russell Simmons

Human nature though, isn't it? Allowing whatever made yesterday a difficult day to cling to us like a big ball of Velcro and stay with us into today! Repeatedly, replaying in our mind who or what made our day hell. Thinking the same thoughts, "What if we had done this, or what if we had done that…" Think about it sensibly for a moment, okay? Can you see how this only makes the present-day hell too, and the day after that, and the day… So, we are going to take a deep breath, mentally agree to whatever it is being left where it belongs, i.e., yesterday, and get on with the day we are in.? Is that a yes? Of course, it is. Bye bye Velcro!

February 20

"The first to apologise is the bravest. The first to forgive is the strongest, and the first to forget is the happiest." ~ *Unknown*

I would like to think that I could be all three, wouldn't you? That would be amazing and would say a great deal about me as a person. However, I must be honest and confess that I find I cannot always be this nice, but I am working on it. I believe that is the only thing most of us can hope to do which is to be the first to be brave, strong, and happy. At least if we are aware that this is what we need to be doing then we are halfway there, so good for us and, if everybody thought the same, well wouldn't that be just wonderful?

February 21

"Do one thing every day that scares you."
~ Eleanor Roosevelt

I don't believe this means to literally scare yourself, but more that you should do something that gets the blood pumping through your veins. Something along the lines of joining a group that you have wanted to join for a while but getting to know a bunch of new people scares you. Or just getting on a bus or train to somewhere you have never been before but have always wanted to explore. Do you get the picture? We all put off or dismiss things we would like to do but may be too scared or nervous to actually act on them. Why hesitate? Resolve to do something out of your comfort zone that scares you. Even if you only do it for a week, a month, won't it be fun and, who knows, what or who it could lead to in the future. BOO!

February 22

"Some people are going to reject you, simply because you shine too brightly for them, and that's okay, keep shining."
~ Dr. Sarah Prevelige

If you are reading this quote you are probably a very Spiritual, sensitive soul and, as such, possess your own "inner light." You may be on your own Spiritual journey and therefore constantly learning and growing in knowledge and becoming comfortable in your own power. In a perfect world everybody you know would be encouraging you and proud of what you are accomplishing. However, in our less-than-perfect world, this is often not the case as one person or people around you may become envious of your newfound wisdom and focus on your life and may gradually distance themselves or indeed may attempt to deter you from continuing on your Spiritual path. Determine to stay focused and do not allow anybody, no matter who they are, to have the power to dim your precious "light."

February 23

"Sometimes you have to move on without certain people. If they're meant to be in your life, they'll catch up." ~ *Mandy Hale*

I believe this is absolutely true for every one of us on our wonderful journey through life. We meet so many people on the way, some at our side the full distance but many others joining us for just a short way before leaving us to continue without them. Personally, I am a great believer that everybody who touches our lives, even for just a moment, does so for a reason. I also believe that, occasionally, someone who has journeyed with us may step off our path and we continue alone. However, if they are meant to, they will step forward to walk by our side in the future, fulfilling our shared destiny for a reason known only to Spirit.

February 24

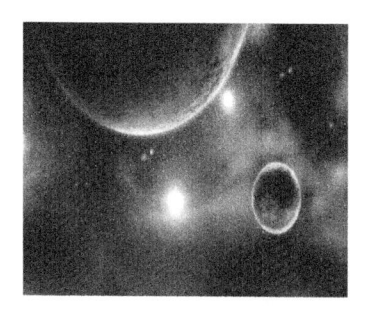

"Without the darkness the stars and moon could not shine." ~ *Unknown*

I don't think I am the only one who enjoys looking at the moon and the stars in the night sky. Isn't it humbling to know that, in the great scheme of things, we are all only tiny, wee specks when compared to the wonders above us? This could also apply to each of us personally in that the sad or troublesome situations we experience, although seeming dark at the time, enable us to appreciate it more when we enjoy happy, carefree times as if the stars and the moon have appeared to show that there is indeed a light of hope out there beyond the darkness.

February 25

"Instead of being afraid to start a new chapter in your life, be as excited as you are when reading a really good book and want to know what happens next. ~ *Unknown*

We all know what it is like to be engrossed in a good book. Longing to turn the page to find out what happens next but, at the same time, realising that you will be one page closer to the end of the story! Life is like a book, isn't it? Made up of chapters we write on our way through it. Some of us are happy with the chapter we are in and choose to stay there for most of the book but some of us, me included, want to write a brand-new chapter for inclusion. How exciting to be able to choose what sort of characters and events to include, and to be able to experiment with new ideas. Of course, there may be uncertainty about how the chapter will end but we are not going to let that stop us from putting pen to paper are we? Of course not. Now, anybody seen my pen...?

February 26

"Some people are going to leave, but that's not the end of your story…. that's the end of their part in your story." ~ *Faraaz Kazi*

I have found this to be very true as I have got older. When I look back, it is easy to see that, although I did not realise it at the time, when people left my life for any reason it was usually because it was the right time for us to walk our separate paths again. We had each taken and given what was necessary from and to each other while we walked the same path. How wonderful! A constant stream of people stepping onto our path to journey beside us, willing to share their lives and time. Some of them, at a time known only to Fate, stepped back onto their own path, leaving us to continue our journey alone. However, there will always be those who wait ahead ready and eager to join us for the next part of our shared journey. So, the cycle continues…

February 27

"If you don't design your own life plan, chances are you'll fall into someone else's plan and, guess what they have planned for you? Not much!" ~ *Jim Rohn*

We are all guilty of just drifting along in life. Occasionally buffeted by the winds of destiny, blown here, blown there, often allowing ourselves to be at the mercy of others. Some of us are fortunate enough to wake up, perhaps due to a well-timed tap from a piece of life's driftwood knocking some sense into us. Each one of us has our own destiny and this relies on us taking charge of our own personal steering wheel of life, charting our course, and keeping to it. I know so many people who have given control of their "wheel" to others who, naturally, are only focused on pursuing their own route/agenda and give no thought to their travelling companion's dreams and aspirations. You have your own "wheel?" Brilliant, off you go then, toot, toot!

February 28

"Don't belittle yourself. Be BIG yourself."
~ Corita Kent

Occasionally, we are our own worst enemies. You know what I mean? Somebody will ask us to do something, and we decline, saying we are not up to it, do not have the confidence, or the skills, yada, yada... The downside is that, if we do this long enough, we start to believe our own hype and our self-confidence takes a nosedive. Much, much better to say, okay, maybe I have not done this before or do not have much experience but, hey ho, I will give it a go. If you keep putting yourself down others will think it's okay to do so too and we don't want to encourage that, do we? However, if you believe in yourself and are willing to at least make an attempt, you can say, "Look out World, here I come!"

February 29

"Try to be a rainbow in someone's cloud."
~ *Maya Angelou*

Now, who would not want to be the rainbow in someone else's cloud? Not me! I can usually sense if the people I encounter every day, whether family, friends, colleagues or just a passing stranger may be experiencing a "cloudy" day in their life, as we exchange a smile or a few words in passing, Of course, this has nothing whatsoever to do with the current weather forecast but to the sense I get that, for whatever reason, they may be feeling troubled. Therefore, I would do my best to help them feel better with a wee chat, a smile, or a hug (I'm a serial hugger remember!) So, wouldn't it be nice to imagine that, when recalling their day at bedtime, they fell asleep with a smile on their face because I became their very own rainbow for just a moment in their cloudy day? Ok, fellow potential rainbows, over to you!

March

March 1

"Remember anyone can love you when the sun is shining. In the storms is where you learn who truly cares for you." ~ *Unknown*

As most of us know, through personal experience, this is absolutely true. We have all had people in our lives who appear quite happy to party with us or join us in carefree pursuits, etc. However, when we reach out during troubling and worrisome times, we may find ourselves scrabbling around in vain trying to locate them. They're not interested in providing a sympathetic ear, monetary assistance, physical aid, or anything else that they would have to put themselves out for in helping us. They disappear until our difficulty has been resolved, only then, reappearing as if by magic to seek us out to reconnect and get the party started again. Time for us to disappear!

March 2

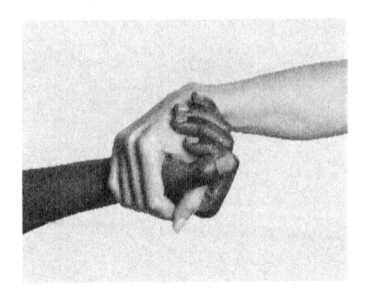

"One acorn can start a forest. One smile can begin peace. One touch can show care. Be that ONE today." ~ *Unknown*

This seems so very apt now with all the terrible things going on in the world today. Most of us wish peace for our fellow human beings who are suffering terribly amid horrendous wars, starvation, or disease. How extremely fortunate we are not to be suffering in the same way. However, the one thing we ARE capable of doing is showing our support in any way we can. Donating food, clothing, money, volunteering our time, it all helps. If each and every one of us could commit to doing at least one of these, can you imagine the tsunami of positivity it would bring to so many lives? Doing rather than talking is a key we all possess. What a difference we could all make in the lives of those so much less fortunate than we are. Click!

March 3

"Live life as if everything is rigged in your favour" ~ *Rumi*

What a wonderful saying! I totally agree and do my best to do what I am told (which does not happen often believe me!). Not so easy though considering the trials and tribulations life has a habit of placing before us on our path, is it? What's the alternative though? Think, "poor wee me," curl into a ball and hide away? Nope! I am reminded of the song "Always look on the bright side of life" which, interestingly, I recently read, is the favourite tune requested at funerals. No more to be said really is there? Now off you go and decide what you want to do next to bring a smile to your face, fill your heart with happiness and add a spring in your step. Boing, boing!

March 4

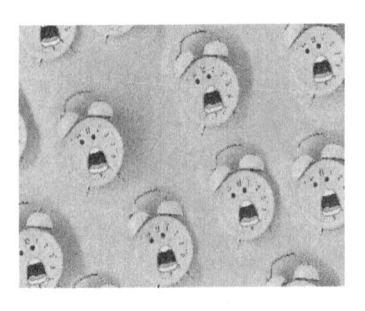

"Love yourself enough to set boundaries. Your time and energy are precious. You get to choose how you use it. You teach people how to treat you by deciding what you will and won't accept." ~ *Anna Taylor*

Are you like I used to be? Prone to being at the beck and call of everybody and everything? Yup, me too! It took me a very long time to learn to say NO when I needed to. In the past, there were those who thought that anytime they needed me to be somewhere, do something, or just adjust my day to revolve around them, all they had to do was whistle. I am now happy to tell you that this changed the day I realised that MY time was precious. Not entirely the other's fault but mine for allowing them to use me this way until it practically became a way of life. One day I "woke" up and decided that I wasn't going to be available or "on call" unless it suited me. It wasn't easy and took a while for everybody to get the message, but I am happy to say that they did!

March 5

"Trying to make someone happy who prefers the drama of being miserable, is a guaranteed way to create your own drama of misery." ~ *Unknown*

Some people are just going to be miserable and view the world and everybody in it as conspirators in a plot to make their existence unbearable. It will not matter how much you do, what you suggest could help, or even just offering a sympathetic ear, whatever. They have no intention of budging from the misery pit they have created and dug themselves into. Trust me, there is no point in trying to pry them loose or throwing them a lifeline, they will resist the former and ignore the latter. You'll only be wasting your precious time and energy so why bother? They may take the opportunity to drag you into the misery pit with them and consequently feel a tad happier because now you are miserable too. Learn when to walk away and leave them to it. You know it's for the best.

March 6

"Nobody else gets to live your life. You're the artist. Paint your own picture. Dream your own masterpiece into being."
~ Barbara Niven

Imagine your life as a blank canvas and what happens to you the brush you paint with. Each stroke has relevance and, once imprinted on the canvas, cannot be corrected or erased. It is totally your personal responsibility for every stroke of the brush you wield. Much will depend on what you accomplish while you create. The people you encounter, the difficulties and disappointments, the joys, and successes, will all make their own mark on your canvas as you journey through life. The brush is yours alone so allow nobody else access in potentially tampering with your creation. Every single one of us is an artist tasked with painting our own life story so let us all strive to make it a masterpiece.

March 7

"Timing is everything. If it's meant to happen it will, at the right time for the right reasons." ~ *Unknown*

People are by nature an impatient species, and some of us more so than others. It seems that everything must be done in a hurry these days, and we want what we want not in the future but NOW, this minute! Being more of an 'erm 'um mature lady nowadays, I have learned through time and experience that things do not necessarily happen when we want them to but when they are meant to in the great scheme of things. It's not always easy to comprehend or understand. However, I've often found, with hindsight, that what happened, happened at exactly the right time, and made perfect sense of what lay ahead. It is all to do with having patience and trusting.

March 8

"Man's law changes with his understanding of man. Only the laws of the Spirit remain always the same."
~ *Native American Crow Proverb*

Our man-made laws are always changing and adapting to the ways in which society is evolving. I believe this can only be a good thing as it means we are paying attention to our laws and how they relate to us in the present day. The laws and rules of Spirit, however, are vastly different and unique. There is no need to change them as the rules of Spirit are similar to those carved in stone and given to Moses. They are based on the eternal truth we all carry within us in our hearts and souls. Such power! Such faith!

March 9

**"If we could look into each other's hearts,
and understand the unique challenges each
of us faces, I think we would treat each
other gently." ~ *Unknown***

*It is a shame, isn't it, that we cannot know what is
going on with somebody unless they choose to tell
us? We can only go by what they allow us to see
which may be a brave face or a "don't care"
attitude. This is what we respond to don't we?
Why shouldn't we? It is their choice, isn't it?
However, it might pay us to delve just a wee bit
deeper and be prepared to offer our help or
understanding, or even just to offer to be there
before making any judgements. We know how they
feel as we have all behaved in this way
occasionally ourselves haven't, we? Time to put
ourselves in their shoes, which have often, on
occasion, also been our shoes, and do what we
can.*

March 10

"Everything you do has the power to change the world. We never know who will be touched by our words or inspired by our actions." ~ *Unknown*

I know that there have been many times in my life when I have been touched or inspired by someone. It may have been something they have written or something they have said or something they have done. Whatever it was, something in me responded. Much of who I am today is the result of the teachings or examples of others and I feel so fortunate and blessed because of it. Blessed, I was aware in realising the gift I was being given, what it had to teach me, and to fully appreciate its worth. How wonderful if I could touch or inspire even one other person in this way! Hopefully, somewhere along the way I have, but I may never know for certain. Will you?

March 11

"When people walk away, let them. Your future is not about people who walk away…. it's about the people who stay in it for the ride." ~ *Unknown*

Sometimes when people want to walk out of our lives, we try to prevent them. Perhaps we believe they still have a part to play therefore we are reluctant to let them go. However, what if they have already played their part and it is the right time for them to leave us? Often, it is not as black and white as this for many of us at the time. Later, on looking back, only then may we be able to acknowledge that they did us a favour by stepping out of our life when they did, although we could not see this at the time. Look around you and appreciate the people who are still walking through life with you because that is where they are meant to be and where you are meant to be at least for the moment.

March 12

"Do not shrink your beautiful light to make someone else feel more comfortable. BE WHO YOU ARE without hesitation, and you will inspire others to shine too."
~ Unknown

I guess we have all been guilty of this at one time or another although it can be human nature not to want to overshadow other people. None of us wants to be perceived as a "show off" do we? However, there is not being a show-off and there is not being true to ourselves by failing to show our personal light. Not being true to ourselves can prevent us from being upfront about our skills or gifts and, by concealing these, others in turn will not learn or be inspired to reach their own goals. It is not in any way showing off to be proud of what you have achieved and thereby inspiring and encouraging others to believe they can do the same.

March 13

If only our eyes saw souls instead of bodies, how very different our ideals of beauty would be." ~ *Lauren Jauregui*

We are a nation, if not a planet, obsessed with how we look and how other people look. I am not afraid to admit that I do not buy popular magazines as they are all crammed with "celebrities," their cosmetically sculpted faces lifted so far up their eyebrows are practically reaching the nape of their neck, and that's just the men! I cannot stand it! What happened to admiring people for what they have achieved in life, their good works, their works of art, literary genius, etc? <u>Not</u> who has had more marriages than anybody else, or who has the most expensive "stuff." Ugh! How interesting and eye-opening it would be if we could see people's souls instead of bodies. I wonder how many "celebrities" would be perceived as beautiful then? Methinks, very few.

March 14

"Each thought and action have the power to brighten or darken MANY lives."
~ Unknown

Being a Water sign I am very in touch with my emotions, too much so at times! I am also very intuitive/empathic regarding other people especially in sensing their emotions. Fortunately, I am insightful enough to be aware of the power I possess to either lift or dash another's feelings. It would hurt me deeply to think I had upset anyone, either by word or deed, therefore I tend to think before I act or speak in relation to the people I encounter in life. I am very thankful for this awareness and insight and realise that not everybody is as fortunate. Wouldn't it be wonderful and make for many more happy people if everyone strove to be this aware?

March 15

"No one said life was easy…. but with great determination, passion, and strength everything is possible." ~ *Unknown*

Oh boy do I know it! I also know I am far from the only one. It is extremely easy for people pummelled by life's boxing gloves to throw in the towel and retreat beaten to their corner. However, where to go from there? Stay cowering in the corner or forever clinging to the ropes for dear life? It is never easy, and nobody is saying it is, to overcome this. However, wouldn't it be to your advantage, in the long run, to climb through the ropes out of the ring and, with your head held high, retreat to the changing room to regain your strength and determination for a return bout? Your next encounter would find you stronger, more determined, and more equipped to succeed in potentially having your arm raised as the winner when the final bell is rung. Ding, ding, ding!

March 16

"When life gets stormy, dance in the rain."
~ Unknown

This always reminds me of the song "Singing In The Rain," from the movie of the same name (1952), with Gene Kelly dancing and singing in the pouring rain with a big smile on his face. Wonderful! They don't make movies like that anymore, sigh.... Now, where was I? Oh yes... I like to think that we could all choose to emulate Gene's determination not to allow the "rain" in his life to dampen his joy in just being alive, aware that the "storm" will pass and there will be sunshine in his life again. So, when you're faced with your own personal storm, and you will, think of Gene. Perhaps refrain from actually dancing and splashing in the rain or you may find yourself in a cosy wee cell being psychiatrically assessed. Enough just to keep in mind that the bad times will pass and keep dancing. Thanks Gene!

March 17

"Don't allow negative people to make you one of them." ~ *Unknown*

Some people are "glass half empty" by nature, aren't they? It doesn't matter how good they have things, or how blessed they are, they always perceive their glass as being half empty and always will. I feel deeply sorry for them as I persist in trying to be a "glass half full" and indeed, a glass hoping to be full again very soon, type of "girl." Being realistic, I tend to let them get on with it as it is their choice, and they are welcome to it. They will never change this "glass half full" lady. I hope you are keeping me company in this belief. Well, are you…?

March 18

"An open mind allows you to explore and create and grow. Remember that progress would be impossible if we always did things the way we always have."
~ Dr. Wayne Dyer

An open mind reminds me of a big plot of land with absolutely nothing remotely resembling a fence on or around it. I guess it could also be that I don't have a lot going on upstairs? Quickly moving on... Those of us who allow our minds to be open to innovative ideas, maintain a thirst for knowledge and seize every opportunity to explore, are the ones responsible for keeping everything moving on the great conveyor belt of life. If we restrict our wonderful minds by mentally erecting and allowing a barrier to sift through all the possibilities moving along our own personal belt and discard anything remotely new, then we are tearing up a treasure map. Be prepared to be open and accepting in adding to your "treasure."

March 19

"Who are you to judge the life I live? I am not perfect and don't have to be! Before you start pointing fingers, make sure your hands are clean." ~ *Bob Marley*

Being honest, I must admit I can occasionally be a tad judgemental, although it is something I am working on. Guilty of being quick to assume or make a snap judgement of someone without knowing anything about them. I am far from alone and most people I know tend to think along the same lines. However, as I said, I am working on it, and learning to take the time to learn a bit more about who someone really is and where they are coming from before I make a judgement. Hopefully, this works both ways and people will take the time to get to know me better or discover more about me before they make snap judgements and form opinions about me and how I should live my life. Quid pro quo rules, okay?

March 20

"Abracadabra is actually a Hebrew word meaning I create what I speak."
~ Unknown

"Abracadabra," what a wonderful word this is, and doesn't it just roll off the tongue? Every child knows that this word, once said, unleashes magic and wonderful things will result. Also reminds me of that other saying "open sesame," it promises to open endless possibilities for magic to create what we most wish for and allow our dreams to come true. We often do not realise that we ARE this wonderful word in our human form and therefore we also have the power to use the magic inside each single one of us to bring our hopes and dreams into being. We are the wand used to create our own special individual magic. Tah, dah!

March 21

"The secret of change is to focus all your energy not on fighting the old, but on building the new." ~ *Socrates*

Being stuck in our ways feels very safe and reassuring to most of us, doesn't it? We know what to expect and how to respond or deal with it. No surprises there then, thank you very much! We often resist change, insisting that the old way of doing things worked out simply fine so why not just continue? Why muddy the water? However, isn't it occasionally wonderful when new opportunities come along and pries us loose from our comfort zone? So, instead of clinging like limpets to the rock of the same old, same old, just let go and swim off into unknown but adventurous waters. How exciting to swim while anticipating reaching a hitherto unexplored shore and discovering all the wonders it has in store for you.

March 22

"A good life is when you assume nothing, need less, do more, smile often, dream big, laugh a lot, and realise how blessed you are for what you have." ~ *Unknown*

That certainly sums up the life we should all be leading or striving to lead. How wonderful and blessed are we if we are already fortunate enough to be living by the message of this quote. I hope I am. I know I do my best to live up to it although, to be honest, it is easier to do some days more than others, but that's ok, at least I got the message. In our busy, occasionally demanding, day-to-day lives it is so easy to forget how blessed we are just to be alive, hopefully fit, and well, and with love in our lives. We truly are blessed compared to many in this poor, beleaguered world of ours. Make sure you take out now and again just to be thankful.

March 23

"Those who dance.... are considered insane by those who cannot hear the music." ~ *George Carlin*

This reminds me of the reaction I occasionally still get when I tell some people I am a professional Tarot and Angel Card Reader. The roll of the eyes, the backing away ever so slightly, the "hmmm, really?" Some even look prepared to make the sign of the cross while reaching for the garlic! They just do not "get" or hear the "music" that I do when I am working with Spirit and my tarot cards. I realise I am truly blessed in being called to work with my cards in providing answers, guidance, insight and resolution for the lovely people who trust me to read for them. As such, being "tuned in" to the music of Spirit and the Universe is truly a gift. Don't you agree it's a great pity we're not all fortunate enough to be "tuned" into the same channel? Maybe one day...

March 24

"If we do not feel grateful for what we already have, what makes us think we'd be happy with more?" ~ *Roy T. Bennett*

We live in a society that appeals to value more what people possess materially rather than what they may lack spiritually. Everything is geared at encouraging us to buy stuff we don't need in order to impress others and make somebody wealthier. We are very much unaware of the constant bombardment of advertising that we are exposed to every single day because it has become part of our daily lives, so we have become accustomed to it. However, step back from it all. Take the time to think about it. Why aren't we satisfied with what we already have? Should we really believe all the hype we are being told? Why do we let them convince us to believe we need more "stuff" to make us happy? We don't, we really don't.

March 25

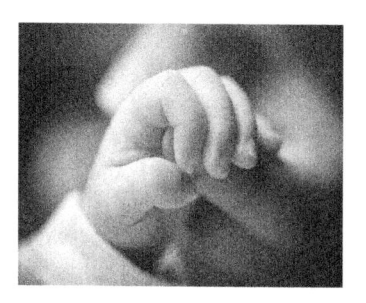

"Stop focusing on how stressed you are and remember how BLESSED you are."
~ Unknown

In our busy everyday lives, it is amazingly easy to get so mired in it that we forget or overlook the many blessings we have. We may be so focused on how stressful our lives are, the irritations, and problems we encounter daily. Often these constantly occupy our every waking thought, and, if we are really unlucky, our dreams offer no escape. It is just how things are in our busy lives and ever-changing world. However, there may be times when we are reminded of the bigger picture; an embrace or kiss from a loved one, the unexpected kindness of a stranger, the laughter of a child, or the suffering caused by an illness. That's when we should realise how blessed we really are and acknowledge and give thanks to whatever Higher Being we personally believe in.

March 26

"Sometimes the bad things that happen in our lives put us directly on the path to the best of things that will ever happen to us."
~ Unknown

This is so true don't you think? Just for an example, I was married in my early 20's to a man who turned out to be a thief and an adulterer. His abusive behaviour caused me to feel battered and bruised emotionally and mentally. However, following my divorce, I met my husband on a blind date through friends and felt we were fated to be together. He is the love of my life, and my rock. A brilliant husband and father, and our wee Oliver and Sienna adore their Grandad.

I believe that events around the troubles in my first marriage ultimately led me to be where I was, in England not Scotland, in order to meet Pete through other people. Whew! Get the message?

March 27

"No matter how big your house is, how new your car is, or how big your bank account is… our graves will always be the same size… stay humble…" ~ *Dalai Lama*

No matter how I try I just do not understand why everything seems to be about how much people have in the way of material possessions? Don't get me started on the obsession people, especially the younger among us, have with "celebrities" and their latest facelift, romance, new handbag, scandal etc. What happened to just being interested in the people around us and being happy to be a part of their lives and content with what we have? We are all going to end up the same way and, as the saying goes, "there are no pockets in a shroud."

March 28

"Having a soft heart in a cruel world is courage, not weakness."
~ *Katherine Henson*

Anybody who knows me will tell you I am a big softy. A sad movie, a heart-wrenching story, being unable to offer help or support to someone in need, it is reach for the tissues time. I used to think this was a sign of weakness and needed to "woman up" as it were but, do you know what, I have changed my mind. Perhaps my tears are because I feel another's pain and suffering but that does not mean I am weak; it just means that I am brave enough to open my heart to another's pain and suffering. Weakness would be closing the doors of my heart to it and thank goodness, that is just not me. Will you be brave too?

March 29

"Life will knock you down. The real learning starts when you have to get back up." ~ *Unknown*

Like me, I expect life has knocked you down a few times if you have been fortunate and a great many times if not. Sometimes, when we feel we have had enough, we may be tempted to just stay down there, asking why we should bother to pick ourselves up just to risk being knocked down again? However, here we are up and willing to give it another go. That is because when we are "down there" hopefully we'd rather be "up there" again and that is our good ole survival instinct kicking in. Every time we continue to grit our teeth and do this, we are learning the lesson of being optimistic and hopeful that things will get better, so good for us eh?

March 30

"Be generous with your blessings. A kind gesture can reach a wound that only compassion can heal." ~ *Steve Maraboli*

Probably most, if not all, of us have been on the receiving end of kindness from another person when we've most needed it. I know I have on many occasions. Not all of us can help those in financial need with a gift of cash, or those without a home or a place to lay their head, etc. However, the one thing we are all more than capable of giving is a kind word, a loving gesture, or offering our support. Often, this is all that is needed to provide comfort and reassurance. The mere fact that someone cares enough to reach out to them with kindness and love may mean more than anything else could at this point in their life.

March 31

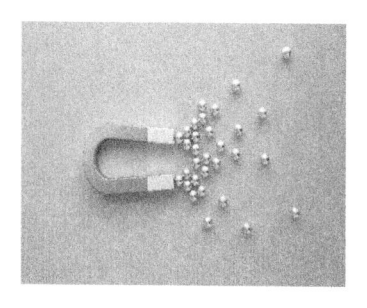

"The more you are thankful for, the more you attract things to be thankful for."
~ Unknown

I always compare this to a ripple in the great pool of life. What starts out as a small pebble (our thanks) thrown into the pool, gradually gets wider and wider the more we throw in and, subsequently, the ripples eventually reach the bank of life where the things or those we need or want lie in wait before gradually being absorbed into the pool. It is all a matter of state of mind. Believe in being thankful for everything in life and trust that the Universe does hear you and acknowledge your gratitude by giving you even more to be grateful for. A win-win situation all round for everybody.

April

April 1

"Silence is a source of great strength."
~ Lao Tzu

Haven't we all, at one time or another, had to bite our tongue to keep quiet because we are in a situation where, if we give vent to what we actually want to say, all hell will break loose? I know I have. However, keep in mind that hurtful words said in anger can never be unsaid. Although not easy, taking time to think before we speak in this kind of situation is the wisest course to take in preventing things from escalating and culminating in a situation there may be no coming back from. Resolving to stay silent is in no way a sign of weakness but rather speaks of great strength.

April 2

"The way people treat you is a statement about who they are as a human being. It is not a statement about you."
~ Jelly (Designer)

Personally, it took me a long time to realise the truth of this. As the Water sign of Pisces, I am very much ruled by my emotions and other people's perceptions of me impacted deeply. Their actions and words could, even unintentionally, make me doubt myself and my abilities and cause my feelings to be hurt. A big softy really! However, I have come to the realisation that everybody has their own story and their own personal dramas in their life, and that sometimes I was just "in the line of fire." Now, as well as being a great deal more confident in who I am, I try to give them the benefit of the doubt in that they are not presently in a good place, so choose to deflect the "fire" and let it go.

April 3

"Everyone you meet is fighting a battle you know nothing about. Be kind, ALWAYS."
~ Brad Meltzer

This is so true and something we all need to be more aware of. I passionately believe that everybody has their own story which has shaped and moulded them into the person they are and that when we encounter each other we need to remember this. It is so easy to respond angrily to another's verbal attack, be impatient with their depressed mood or tendency to look on the dark side, when we are unaware of what they are going through. If we can, and I say "if," look past their tendency to lash out in anger, and show patience, understanding and kindness, this may be all that is needed to help them feel better and able to deal with their problems. Therefore, wouldn't it make more sense to make the effort?

April 4

"When you face difficult times, know that challenges are not sent to destroy you. They're sent to promote, increase, and strengthen you." ~ *Joel Osteen*

Usually when trouble visits us it never just comes once, but two or three times, just to make sure we get the message that we are having difficulties. One visit is bad enough, but more than that and we are left wondering "Why me?" or "It's not fair," and generally hard done by. However, time passes, and somehow or other we get through usually just because we must. Sometime later may come the realisation that what happened worked out for the best by showing us how strong we are in coping and instilling a newfound confidence we did not possess previously to sustain us in the future.

April 5

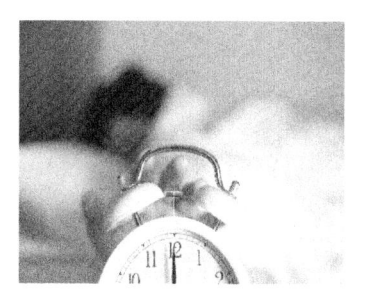

"I didn't change. I just woke up!"
~ *Unknown*

This very much resonates with me regarding my Spiritual awakening and what it has led to since. Working, being a wife and a mum, a cousin, aunt and friend, meant the people in my life always saw me in this role for many years. A role I cherished and still do. When I began to collaborate with Spirit in, I believe, my true calling, they were incredibly surprised at how much I had "changed" when all I felt was relief and contentment in actually being "me" at last, growing into who I was meant to become. A true awakening and a very welcome one but something everybody else has had to get used to.

❧

April 6

"I accept myself for who I am and what I believe. It is not my responsibility for you to accept me. That is your problem."
~ Unknown

It has taken an exceptionally long time, but I believe I am now doing what I was meant to. However, initially, not everybody was as accepting of the path I had chosen as I had thought. All to do with a family member's religious belief as opposed to my belief in Spirituality. However, in the end, we agreed to disagree with one another and left it at that with no difference in the feelings we have for each other. I would never consider criticising anyone's religious beliefs or customs and would hope and expect the same courtesy extended to mine.

April 7

"There is not ONE path. There is not even the RIGHT path. There is only YOUR path." ~ *Unknown*

This should be instilled in every human being from birth! A saying and tenet to live by don't you think? If everybody genuinely believed this with all their heart, perhaps the world would be a much happier, safer, harmonious place for us all. Unfortunately, for humanity, I don't see this happening any time soon. Perhaps, if this message could be put "out there" more widely and circulated as far as possible, I wonder how many lives it could potentially alter for the better?

April 8

"I am the most powerful tool in my life, and I will use me wisely." ~ *Unknown*

This is true for each and every one of us. Our minds and bodies are ours to use to mine and extract what we want and need from life. When you really think about it, how amazing are we? Our bodies and brains are able to work in harmony, enabling us to live, work, play, interact, deduce, etc., with few restrictions apart from the ones we place on ourselves. It behooves us to use the capabilities we have emotionally, as well as physically and spiritually, with as much determination as we can possibly muster. No downing tools for us any time soon, no sir!

April 9

"Forget all the reasons it won't work and believe the one reason that it will."
~ Ziad K. Abdelnour

We are all guilty of this aren't we? Thinking about starting something new or wanting to expand on what we are already doing and then the doubts creep in.... Then it is, "what if.... but maybe...am I good enough.... what do I do if it fails?" Sound familiar? Of course, it does. We have all been there at one time or another. It is healthy and makes sense to consider what could happen before we launch ourselves into whatever project we have in mind but, and here is the thing, we also must start believing in ourselves and our ability to reach a positive outcome. Just finding one reason to "go for it" can make all the difference between thinking and doing.

April 10

"What is, is. What isn't, isn't. You become so obsessed with what isn't that you miss what is." ~ *Aristotle*

Exactly! How true is this? Basically, what this means is that occasionally we allow ourselves to focus on what hasn't happened in our lives, i.e., a great job, the loving fulfilling relationship, winning the lottery, etc. All this does is stop us from getting on with life. Perhaps, by making the best of what we have, we can achieve what we dream of, perhaps not winning the lottery, but seeking out and pursuing better job opportunities, the possibility of finding that special someone etc. Doesn't that make more sense?

April 11

"You never know how strong you are until being strong is the ONLY option you have left." ~ *Ziad K. Abdelnour*

Interesting, don't you think? We often find ourselves in stressful or upsetting situations obviously not through choice, but because that's life, things just happen. Most times, although there's momentary panic and indecision, we determine to pull ourselves together and do what we must as best we can. This may involve asking for help from those more qualified in finding a solution. We never realise how strong we really are until, unfortunately, we are in the midst of a crisis. It's then, and only then, that making the decision to be strong rather than buckle, is the one thing we can do to the best of our ability.

April 12

"Courage doesn't always roar. Sometimes courage is the quiet voice at the end of the day, saying I will try again tomorrow."
~ Mary Anne Radmacher

Just a reminder I guess that having and showing courage does not necessarily mean everybody knows about it, because we are putting it out there. It is more to do with having a really difficult day but, before going to sleep, we silently reassure ourselves that, you know what, I'm not giving up. I am going to give it another go tomorrow and, with that thought in our mind, allow sleep to claim us. Being courageous just means being afraid but never ever giving up.

April 13

"Peace begins with a smile. Every time you smile at someone, it is an action of love, a gift to that person, a beautiful thing."
~ Mother Teresa

It surprises me sometimes that I have not either been locked up or verbally abused because I tend to smile at people wherever I find myself. Walking up the street, in shops, bus queues etc., you name it, I have probably been there smiling at all and sundry. I think most people on the receiving end of a smile from me just naturally find themselves smiling back. I like to think that, even if that is the only smile or personal interaction they have that day, even just from a total stranger, that it has made their life brighter just for that short exchange. It gives me something too so why not try it yourself and see what happens?

April 14

**"Logic will get you from a to b.
Imagination will take you everywhere."
~ *Albert Einstein***

Logic is fine and, of course, it has a significant role to play in our lives and can be a great asset in the way we need to look at and consider certain things. However, letting loose our imagination is like freeing a bird within us, allowing us to soar, explore and roam wherever we want. No limit or restraints involved, just total freedom, how wonderful is that? It is up to each and every one of us to choose to allow and encourage our "bird" to go to places or situations our logical mind would be shaking its head and wagging an admonitory finger at us for! Go on, where will your "bird" fly today?

April 15

"Be yourself….no matter what other people think. God made you the way you are for a reason. Besides, an original is always worth more than a copy." ~ *Unknown*

I believe this is something some of us find exceedingly difficult or uncomfortable in just being who we are. We tend to want people to think the best of us so find ourselves going along with their ideas or suggestions when we actually want to scream "No!" It takes courage for us to be strong in ourselves when it comes to expressing our own opinion, not just going along with someone else's, or defending our beliefs from attack. However, think about it…. does it make us feel better being one of the herd? Of course, it won't. Much better to be true to who our Creator meant us to be, a genuine original, a one-off, rather than a paltry copy.

April 16

"Strength doesn't come from what you can do. It comes from overcoming the things you once thought you couldn't."
~ Rikki Rogers

It does not take strength to do what we do every day as normally it involves just going along with whatever we have planned in order to earn a living, run a household, a social life etc. We do what we know we must because that is what life usually entails, just getting on with it. Strength comes into play when things do not go the way we expect or want, and we doubt ourselves in being able to cope and overcome successfully. So much easier for us to ignore or expect someone else to sort things out for us. However, finding the strength to do it ourselves this time enables us to cope better the next time, and the next..........

April 17

"Don't expect only happiness in your life. There are going to be dark times but remember that stars need darkness to shine." ~ *Unknown*

I believe a great many of us realise that life tends not to be one continual path of round of continual happiness but a combination of both happiness and despair, Also, unfortunately for many of us, in unequal measures. However, that's life and there is nothing we can do about it but accept and do our best to cope and move on from the unhappy times. The only good thing, if there is such a thing, is that the unhappy times should bring us the realisation that the happy times need to be enjoyed and treasured. Just like the stars need darkness to shine, so the happy times need the unhappy times to make us value them as we should.

April 18

"Each new moment is a place you've never been." ~ *Unknown*

Absolutely true, isn't it? We do not often stop to think about this though, do we? Too much going on, too many things to do, people to see, places to go... Take a moment to think about it. Each new moment in your life is unique to you and only to you. Once it has gone it is gone, never to return but has created another small stitch in the tapestry of your life that is an ongoing work of art, your own personal masterpiece! Appreciate the moment before you bid it farewell to the needle forever...

April 19

"If you want to see a miracle, just open your eyes. Everywhere you look, there's magic in disguise." ~ *Unknown*

Oh, there is, there is! Take time to appreciate the miracles around you all the time, every day. A new baby, a flower, even the rain that we often complain about but without which everyone and everything on our planet would perish. True miracles are to be found in nature. People being kind, caring and thoughtful towards others. The list is endless. True magic is to be discovered in all of these and much more. It is up to each one of us to notice and appreciate the magic enhancing our own lives and the lives of those we love.

April 20

"If you want to fly, you have to give up the things that weigh you down."
~ *Toni Morrison*

No, this does not mean, taking off overcoats or heavy shoes, tut tut! This is all about letting go of all the restrictions or self-doubts we tend to take on board in life and freeing ourselves. We tend to add "weights" to ourselves in the form of low self-belief, self-esteem, or self-confidence. Perhaps even allowing other people to burden us with their unhelpful perceptions of us. Now, how are we going to spread our wings and "fly" with all that weighing us down? We are not, therefore, like the sandbags in the basket of our hot air balloon, we must hoist them over the side and watch them disappear, hopefully missing the people below! Now our Spirits have the freedom to find and bring us what we wish for most.

April 21

"You don't stop dancing because you grow old, you grow old because you stop dancing." ~ *Mark Twain*

I love this! I know that, with my creaky and achy joints, I am not as supple or as pain free as I was when I was, 'er ahem, much younger. However, what am I going to do? Never dance again when I hear music I want to boogie to? (Apologies to my children for the unwelcome images they now have in their heads.) I do not think so! If that day ever comes, and it never will if I can help it, then I will feel a profound sense of loss and know I have indeed got old. Until then, much to the amusement of those unfortunate enough to witness me boogieing, I will continue to let the music "take me!"

April 22

"When you change the way you look at things, the things you look at change."
~ Wayne Dyer

I think we can all relate to this. We tend to form an opinion or judge people very quickly, occasionally unfavourably, without knowing all the facts or spending time getting to know them. This judgement in our minds takes root and is filed away for future reference. However, if we can just take steps to get to know people better before forming an opinion, then we may find ourselves forming a totally different perception of them. This, in turn, may change them into somebody you find yourself valuing as a friend, colleague or lover in the future. Trust me, snap judgements are not a good idea.

April 23

"Only you can fill in what's missing. It's not something another person can do for you."
~ Haruki Murakami.

Have you ever had the feeling that something is "missing" in your life? I am not talking about someone, but a feeling, a belief, something that resonates with your very Spirit or soul. I believe we each seek out what we feel drawn to and that this enriches and enables us to feel comfortable, happy, and content with who and where we are in life. Those of us who have achieved this are extremely fortunate indeed to have realised that nobody but ourselves could "fill in what was missing" and acted accordingly. I hope you have found or find the same.

April 24

"Moving forward away from your comfort zone may feel temporarily uncomfortable, but it feels a lot better than standing still in a place that no longer suits you."
~ Unknown

It is only natural to construct our own personal comfort zone as a cushion or buffer protecting us from the impact life and the world can have on us. It is where we feel most comfortable and from where we can direct our life. However, our comfort zone will change and evolve as we experience and deal with life and that, after a while, it may not be as comfortable as it once was. Hopefully, if this happens, we will be realistic and brave enough to move on and discover what the future has in store for us.

April 25

"A good friend finds you in the dark and carries you back to the light." ~ *Unknown*

I am very blessed in life in having many friends who, I know, I could rely on totally if I was suddenly plunged into the darkness of despair, through unexpected events in my life. This knowledge brings me great comfort and peace. My friends are also aware that this works both ways, and I would not hesitate to do the same for them. I hope you all have that special person or people in your life who are prepared to brave their fear of the dark to find you and carry you back to the light.

April 26

"Worrying does not take away tomorrow's troubles, it takes away today's peace."
~ *Randy Armstrong*

This is absolutely true isn't it, but it is something we all do nevertheless! We all have worry "buttons" some of us smaller or larger than others. We worry about everything, occasionally over nothing very much but, at other times, we have good reasons for worrying. Once that seed of worry takes root in our head nothing will shift it, so it stays there, making its presence known. Great if we could solve it easily and consign it to the worry waste basket. Not so great if seems unsurmountable. However, if we need to worry, it is much better to worry about tomorrow's worry tomorrow rather than allow it to destroy the peace of today.

April 27

There is no path to happiness. Happiness is the path." ~ *A.J. Muste*

Exactly! I could not have said it better myself. Allow happiness to live within and around you as you travel your path in life. Forget trying to find the path to where you think you will find it and instead look within yourself. Each of us is capable of finding and realising our own personal version of what makes us happy so wouldn't it benefit us to just concentrate on this rather than spending valuable time searching for something we already possess?

April 28

"Pay attention to whatever inspires you, for it is "Spirit" trying to communicate with you. That's why it's called "inspiration" as "inspirit." Listen to it, believe it, and act on it." ~ *Unknown*

Basically, this asks that we aren't too prepared to dismiss those "coincidences," signs, synchronicities we may experience in life. Instead, acknowledge them for what they are and act accordingly. It may be Spirit trying to catch your attention and make you aware of someone or something or an action you need to take. I love it when this happens because it is validation that a "higher power" has you in its sights and is attempting to make something known to you by giving you signs or nudges in the right direction. How special does that make you feel? So never ignore whatever your "gut" is telling you but look forward to something exciting coming forward.

April 29

"Your vision will become clear only when you look into your heart. Who looks outside, dreams. Who looks inside, awakens." ~ *Carl Jung*

We all have dreams we want realised in our lives and strive to make these a reality and not just something in our head. Something to aim and hope for can be vital in giving us reasons to keep going through the not so good times. A life without dreams would be a poor life indeed. However, it would pay us to look deep within ourselves, our very Spirit, to discover our true goals or reasons to keep going. This deeper insight may be the tool we use to awaken our sense of who we really are and what we need to awaken us from the sleep of unawareness.

April 30

"Be happy for no reason, like a child. If you are happy for a reason, you're in trouble because that reason can be taken from you." ~ *Deepak Chopra*

Much easier said than done, don't you think, being happy for no reason? Surely, our happiness depends on reasons presenting themselves and triggering feelings of happiness in us? I feel it is more that children are not encumbered, as we adults may tend to be, with the worries of daily life, but just take the day as it comes without worrying or stressing about what it may bring. Wonderful, eh? Oh, that we could be like that again! We have learned over time, however, that the people or things that bring happiness into our lives can, through unforeseen or unexpected circumstances, be taken away from us. It would therefore pay us, if we could, to be happy just for the sake of being happy.

May

136

May 1

"Do what you can with what you have, where you are." ~ *Theodore Roosevelt*

Oh, I do! Hopefully, you do too? Realistically, that is all any of us can do, isn't it? Nothing else for it but to get on with things. It would be great to think that every one of us realises the gifts we were born with and the abilities and skills we have gained on our way through life. Then, equipped with this knowledge, do the best we can, not only to enrich our lives, but also the lives of those around us. Who knows the gifts we may be able to give to each other!

May 2

"If you want to feel rich…just count the things you have that money can't buy."
~ Zig Ziglar

Sometimes we are so caught up and swept along by the things we have to do every day that we never take the time to stop and think about the many blessings we have in life that we take for granted. I don't mean the 50" Smart TV, the posh car, the expensive clothes, etc. I mean the blessings we are fortunate enough to have been given for free, i.e., our health and the health of those we love, a happy home, people in our lives who love us for who we are, financial stability, being able to appreciate the world around us and its beauty… Too many blessings to mention so I will leave you to reflect on your own personal blessings for which I am sure you are truly thankful.

May 3

"To be yourself in a world that is constantly trying to make you something else is the greatest achievement." ~ *Deborah Doris Fell*

Have you noticed the constant bombardment of advertising we are exposed to daily? We all have access to the wider world thanks to modern technology and this can be a good thing, enabling us to interact with other people, in other parts of the country or the world. Also, keeping us up to date with what is happening around this wonderful planet of ours. However, we are also allowing into our homes, offices, leisure pursuits, those who want to sell us something we do not really need, things we cannot really afford, the opportunity to create debts by purchasing "stuff." Take no notice of what you do not have to and stay who you are not who somebody else thinks you should be.

May 4

"You are the only real obstacle in your path to a fulfilling life." ~ *Les Brown*

Absolutely true, but how many of us are aware enough to realise it! It is extremely easy to doubt that we do possess our own unique abilities and skills and may instead tend to believe that everybody else is cleverer, more talented, more uniquely gifted, etc? What we fail to realise is that they are probably thinking the same about us! Discard the blinkers forever and have faith in yourself. Do not be the one who denies you the opportunity(s) to follow your dreams! Be the one who encourages and inspires you to just go for it and see what happens!

May 5

Don't cry because it's over, smile because it happened." ~ *Dr. Seuss*

I am sure we have all, at one time or another, had a failed relationship, an unfulfilled dream, a disappointment etc. At that time, it usually feels like the end of the world, doesn't it? We tell ourselves we will never love that way again. That's it, no more dreams. I am not willing to risk another disappointment.... The amazing thing though is that many of us find, as time passes, our memories change and we can look back, with hindsight, and realise that whatever happened did, in fact, provide us with the key to another opportunity with greater potential. We are then able to allow ourselves a smile in recollection and give thanks that, although it pained us at the time, things turned out for the best.

May 6

"You create your thoughts. Your thoughts create your intentions, and your intentions create your reality." ~ *Wayne Dyer*

This makes sense! We do create our thoughts, don't we? So, let's each one of us, from this moment on, take a silent oath that every uplifting thought we have, we use to create the best intentions we possibly can, thus ensuring that our realities become what we want them to be. Then determine to use these to the best of our ability to shape and guide our future path through life. Who is with me?

May 7

"Human beings can alter their lives by altering their attitudes of mind."
~ *William James*

I think this is one of those things that not many of us take the time to think about, i.e., just how major an impact our own attitudes have on, not only our lives, but the people who populate it. The brain is the "steering wheel" propelling us through life. So, doesn't it make sense to use this the best way we can by ensuring that we are heading in the best and most advantageous direction for us? By discarding previously perhaps uncompromising or outdated beliefs we begin to alter the "road" we travel thus freeing us to reach a more hospitable and promising destination. Vroom, vroom!

May 8

"Everything flows and nothing stays."
~ Heraclitus

This is so, so true, not just for us, but for everything. Every human being, every living thing, the earth, the seasons, absolutely everything is moving constantly second by second. Nothing is the same as it was only a moment ago, including us. How many times have you revisited somewhere you lived or visited previously and were taken aback by the way it had altered since you last saw it? The same with people, isn't it? You meet someone you have not seen for years and silently think "My goodness they've got older" not realising they are thinking the same about you! There is nothing we can do to slow or halt this natural process which has been going on since the beginning of time, so much better just to go with the flow don't you think?

May 9

"As you breathe in, cherish yourself. As you breathe out, cherish all beings."
~ *Dalai Lama*

I can just picture this, can't you? Breathing in life-sustaining air to nourish our bodies and, just a tad more important, helping keep us alive. Then, breathing out and picturing with our mind's eye our very breath of life being expelled and set free to enhance and nourish everyone and every living thing around us. A precious gift freely given from us to whoever needs it most. What a gift eh?

May 10

"Some people are hurting so bad you have to do more than preach a message to them. You have to be a message to them."
~ Joyce Meyer

I interpret this as meaning that sometimes when we are called upon to be there to support, comfort or encourage a friend in need, words are not enough. Although we mean well and can all verbalise the platitudes that we all use at these times, you know what, maybe all they need is to know is that we ourselves are conveying a message of comfort and hope just by being by their side when they most need to know we are there for them. Be prepared to be a message of hope when you need to be and, hopefully, when we are in need, they will be the message of hope for us.

May 11

"When the caterpillar thought it was the end of the world, it turned into a butterfly."
~ *Deepak Chopra*

What a lovely picture that conjures up doesn't it? A tiny caterpillar shedding its outer skin and emerging transformed as a beautiful, colourful, fragile butterfly. We are remarkably similar in that we go about our daily lives totally ignorant of just how special every one of us is in the great scheme of things. Perhaps something unexpected happens and turns everything upside down for us and plunges us into the depths of despair and uncertainty about what will happen next. This is when we find we have the ability to cope and turn things back around and realise that, while doing so, we have morphed into a beautiful butterfly.

May 12

"Today is your day to let go of things that no longer serve you." ~ *Unknown*

We periodically go through our wardrobes, closets, etc., and have a good clear out of the things that we no longer want to keep because we know we will never find a need for them in the future, or they no longer bring us what they once did. If you take the time to think about it, the same can be said for certain people, places, groups in our lives, can't it? When was the last time that you had a good "clear out?" Perhaps your life would be richer and freer if you were prepared to let go of people or things that serve no useful purpose for you? Think about it.

May 13

"Be with someone who brings out the best in you, not the stress in you." ~ *Unknown*

Most of the people we surround ourselves with are there because we want them to be and, indeed, actively encourage their presence in our lives. However, I know we all have, or have had, people in our lives who, just by hearing their voice on the 'phone, anticipating their visit, or invited to meet up, cause us to feel anxious and stressed. Especially those who spend the whole time you are together talking about themselves with nary a word asking how you are. Why do it to ourselves? Let us all strive to surround ourselves with people who do bring out the best in us not the stress in us by only accepting the invitations of those we DO want to spend time with!

May 14

"Certain things catch your eye but pursue only those that capture the heart."
~ *Native American Proverb*

There is certainly much out there to catch our eye isn't there? Whether it is on TV, bill posters, social media, etc., it is impossible not to constantly be aware in noticing what is around us. Indeed, we live in a consumer-obsessed world surrounded by hype urging us to buy things we do not really need, sign up to deals that profit other people, or promoting ways we can be more or look more like so called "celebrities." These things are transient, they have no substance, and they are unrealistic... Try to look past all this and then you will see the true beauty that is out there, within your grasp. The love of family, true friendships, the beauty to be found by just looking around and being aware of the miracle of nature and the animals inhabiting this wonderful world of ours.

All we need to enrich our hearts and souls for the taking with no price tag attached.

May 15

"A heart that reaches out with love can heal a soul and change a life."
~ *Kiran Shaikh*

Many of us do not realise just how powerful love is and the magic of which it is capable. Isn't it wonderful and empowering to be aware that we all possess this magic within us and are free to choose how we use it? Love is born within us as we emerge into this world of ours and, if we are fortunate, we are brought up surrounded by the love of those around us. There will be many times throughout our lives when we can, by using this love, heal those who suffer and even change their lives forever for the better. Such power, such responsibility, such willingness to reach out and give freely……

May 16

**"Your mind is not a cage. It is a garden...
and it requires cultivating."** ~ *Libba Bray*

Doesn't this make perfect sense? Our mind is only a cage if we allow it to be and therefore why would we choose to do that to ourselves? Like a garden, our mind nourishes and grows only what we choose to "plant" in it. We also have the ability to "weed" when necessary and pluck out and discard those things growing that we realise serve no purpose or, indeed, hold us back or hinder us in the cultivation of our fertile, expanding mind.

May 17

"A tree that is unbending is easily broken."
~ Lao Tzu

Now this is quite straightforward, isn't it? We all know that trees are usually planted deeply and firmly in order to grow strong and sturdy, don't we? However, when a gale-force wind blows, and the tree fails to "give" in order to cope there is every chance that the wind will persevere until the tree is just ripped from the earth by its roots and blown whichever way the wind chooses. Like the beautiful trees, we will face many, many times in life when we are buffeted by situations, people, or stress, and if we do not bend and adapt when dealing with these, we too may be broken in Spirit and cast adrift.

May 18

"Remembering a wrong is like carrying a burden in the mind." ~ *Buddha*

Easier said than done! When somebody does us wrong, we tend to brood and allow it to fester and grow in our mind. Over time, if we refuse to let it die a natural death and fade away never to be thought of again, like a boil or a carbuncle it grows and grows and grows.... We continue to feed it from a menu of anger, vengeance, and our sense of injustice. Now, is this doing anything to the person who caused it? Of course, it isn't! All this does is torment and prevent us from thinking clearly and getting on with our lives content and at peace. Let it go, just let it go, you do not need it, really you don't!

May 19

"A wise owl lived in an oak, the more he saw the less he spoke, the less he spoke the more he heard. Why can't we all be like that wise old bird?" ~ *Charles M. Shultz*

Personally, I love owls. There is just something about them that appeals to me. They always look comfortable in their own feathers if you know what I mean? This quote really resonates with me and, as it makes a lot of sense, there is not much I can add except to adopt what it is telling us. Sometimes we need to just listen and engage our brains while learning and digesting what we hear before opening our mouths and letting it all out without really knowing what we are saying or mean. Perhaps we would hear things to our advantage, who knows? Worth a try.

May 20

"Transformation happens on the other side of surrender." ~ *Unknown*

We have all struggled with problems in the past and, most of the time, done our utmost to find a solution, a way to move forward and leave whatever it is behind. However, occasionally, very occasionally, there are times when we should just say, "You know what, I give up. That's it. I can do no more." At those times perhaps that is just the way we are meant to react to whatever, or whoever, is causing us a problem. By admitting and accepting that we don't know the best way forward, can allow the dust to settle, and we are then ready to be transformed into the person who accepts and allows things to happen and trust that what follows is for the best.

May 21

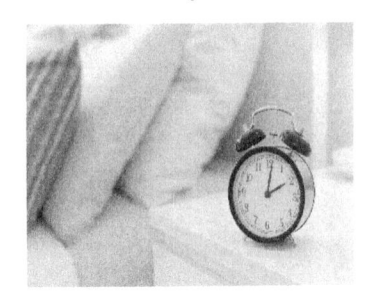

"Wake up with determination. Go to bed with satisfaction." ~ *Dawn Abraham*

Personally, I wake up every morning thankful for actually waking up! Joking aside, how many of us wake up and spend a minute or two thinking about the day ahead with something less than anticipation? From today, when you wake up, try to picture your day ahead and feel determined to get the absolute best out of the entire day you can! This should find you starting your day with anticipation and an eagerness that will carry you through the following hours and bring, not only to you, but to the people you encounter and interact with, a sense of wellbeing, cheerfulness, and positive energy. So, by the time you climb back into bed and snuggle down you fall asleep with a smile on your face in anticipation of the next day being much the same.

May 22

"Let your faith be bigger than your fear."
~ *Unknown*

If only it were that easy! Sometimes our fears are very, very scary, and deeply rooted, and it is almost impossible for us to look beyond them to the light at the end of the tunnel. However, saying that, what if, when we are fearful, just, closing our eyes, taking deep breaths, finding the calm in our core and "letting go." This is when we should tap into our belief in whichever faith we follow. Allow the peace we are all capable of surrounding ourselves with, if we choose, to take us over and just trust. A short but lovely word, trust. Try it the next time you are fearful, you may be surprised!

May 23

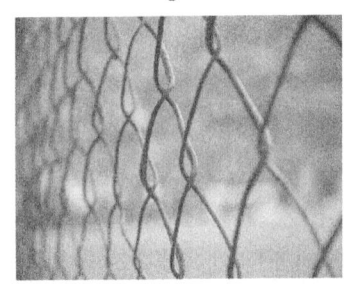

**"Care about what other people think of you
and you will always be their prisoner."**
~ Lao Tzu

*I can certainly see the logic in this, can't you?
Self-explanatory, although I suspect we have all
been guilty of this at one time or another in our
lives. Perhaps many of us continue to be! We may
subconsciously or not seek other people's
approval of what we do and, indeed, who we are.
Not realising we are allowing them control over
us and how we live our lives and, in fact, present
ourselves to the World. Try doing what YOU want
to do, the way YOU want to, how YOU want to,
and you may be surprised at how liberated you
feel, perhaps for the first time in an exceedingly
lengthy period. Refuse to be anyone's prisoner
ever again.*

May 24

**"Breathing in, I send myself love.
Breathing out, I send love to someone else
who needs it." ~ *Buddha***

Wonderful, isn't it? Breathing in we send ourselves life-giving oxygen, which we don't often stop to think about do we? We just do it as it comes to us as naturally as breathing, if you know what I mean? We are continually nourishing our life-force if you like. Also, what if we held the intent that every time, we breathed out we were able to send love to someone in need of it. Wouldn't it be amazing to be able to send out healing and restorative love with each breath so, not only nourishing us, but also those who need it most? Wonderful!

May 25

"When I accept myself, I am freed from the burden of needing you to accept me."
~ Steve Mariboli

Accepting ourselves means being happy and confident that we know who we are and what we, not only want from life, but what we are prepared to give to life. We are realistic about our personal imperfections and shortcomings but aware these are necessary in shaping us to become members of the human race. This realisation also enables us to be free from the restrictions others may attempt to impose on us. However, not all of us are this fortunate, perhaps through another's interventions or actions, to be able to do this. The first step to being free to be who you are, is to be aware and admit that you are NOT free and consequently take the steps you need to rectify this.

May 26

"Everything we do is infused with the energy with which we do it. If we're frantic, life will be frantic. If we are peaceful, life will be peaceful." ~ *Marianne Williamson*

We are motivated by energy, and this is what drives us every day of our lives, in everything we do and quite rightly so or we would never get anything done. However, there's energy and there's frantic energy! If we are frantic all the time, sure, we get things done quickly and probably appear to accomplish more in a shorter period but let us look at this realistically. Allowing ourselves to be totally driven by an out of control, impetuous, unstructured, unimpeded energy exposes us to the risk of being totally overwhelmed. It would make more sense, wouldn't it, to pace ourselves in allowing our energy to work for us in a calm, focused, straightforward way enabling us to go through life more peacefully which, let's face it, is the only way to go.

May 27

"As I declutter my life, I free myself to answer the calling of my soul." ~ *Unknown*

It took me many years to realise I needed to declutter my life, not only materially, but also physically and mentally. So, began a gradual process of "weeding." Over time, I began to feel less encumbered and weighed down. As this progressed, I began to experience a Spiritual awakening which, as time has gone by, has brought me new friends, enlightening experiences, a great many opportunities to learn more about what I feel is my calling, and a purpose to my life. It has taken me a wee while, but I am gradually getting there and believe my soul has breathed a sigh of relief. If you haven't already, why don't you try "decluttering" and see what happens? I think you will be surprised by the results.

May 28

"If you are depressed you are living in the past. If you are anxious you are living in the future. If you are at peace you are living in the present." ~ *Lao Tzu*

Not easy to follow this one, is it? No matter how good our intentions are, the past will persist in intruding and tormenting us with past mistakes, wrong decisions, etc. As if that were not enough to stress us out, worries about the future keep us awake at night, conjuring up various scenarios for disaster that may lie ahead, arghh! Ok, so the most sensible thing for me to do, is leave the past where it is as there is nothing, I can do to change it so that's sorted. There is also nothing I can do about the future as, hopefully, it will all work out as I have planned but, if not, well I will worry about that at the time. Now, regarding the present, this is something I can do something about and therefore I consciously choose to allow myself to live in peace, taking each day as it comes and dealing with it accordingly.

May 29

"Dance like no one is watching. Love like you'll never be hurt. Sing like no one is listening. Live like it's Heaven on Earth."
~ William Purkey

I love this and try to adopt this in my life. It is also inspiring to see that this philosophy is appearing more frequently in the media, especially as it appears to be aimed at those of us who are not 'er ahem, in the first flush of youth! I do think that more of us of the older generation are taking this advice on board and dancing like no one is watching (or even if they are), love like we'll never be hurt (even though we may be), and sing like no one is listening (which, trust me, wouldn't be pleasant if they did listen to me!) In fact, enjoy your life. Do what YOU want to do, what you feel would make YOU happy, and see what happens.... go on, you know you want to!

May 30

"If you light a light for someone else…it will also brighten your path." ~ *Unknown*

Being able to "light a light" for someone else is what I love most about reading for people. Many of the people who come to me for a reading are often very troubled souls. They appear weighed down by whatever problems they are experiencing and seem unable to see any hope for their future. At the beginning of the reading they sat, slouched, and slumped before me, shoulders drooping with the cares of the world showing on their faces. Then the reading begins… As I channel Spirit and the reading unfolds and they receive reassurance that things will improve, problems will resolve, they will find love in their lives, etc., they begin to bloom again. When the reading ends and they leave me with hugs and a spring in their step for perhaps the first time in a lengthy period, I am also uplifted and filled with joy in doing what I love most in working for and with Spirit.

May 31

"Those who deserve love the least, need it the most." ~ *Austin O'Malley*

Occasionally, people are their own worst enemies. You know what I mean. People we come across in our day-to-day lives who appear to take pleasure in alienating or upsetting those around them, just for the sake of it. Very frustrating for us as we can see no valid reason for their behaviour other than to cause mischief or upset. However, it might pay us to look more deeply at what they themselves are experiencing in their own lives at the time. We all react differently to problems, worries or stress, and this is their way of coping or showing distress by hitting out at those closest to them. The next time somebody is causing you grief, before you respond in anger, try taking the time to sit down and talk to them. Try to discover what may be causing their behaviour and you may begin to understand why they are behaving the way they are. Try love before anger, it may just work.

June

168

June 1

"Blessed are those who can give without remembering and take without forgetting."
~ Elizabeth Bibesco

I can imagine this is the type of person we all aspire to and believe ourselves to be. You know what I mean, we can give freely with no strings attached, no hidden agenda, and then forget about it, happy just to have been able to help. However, when we ourselves need some help, either emotionally or financially, we never forget who gave freely to us and ensure we always carry this with us and repay our debt should the opportunity present itself.

June 2

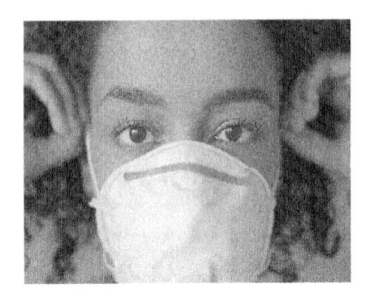

"The most common form of despair is not being who you are." ~ *Soren Kierkegaard*

Hopefully, most of us, including me, live our lives totally in tune with who we are and therefore feel totally free to express our feelings and opinions openly without fear of criticism or censure. Sadly, there are those among us who are filled with despair because they may feel that this freedom is not possible for them, either due to society's dictates or by their own choices or constraints. How sad must that be for them? I can only imagine their sadness and despair. If any of you know someone like this, wouldn't it be great to help them shake off their despair and join the rest of us in living life just who we are? Not much to ask really, is it?

June 3

"I am thankful for those difficult people in my life. They have shown me who I do not want to be." ~ *Unknown*

Oh, dear me, yes definitely! We have all known people like this or, unfortunately, still do! Do you know who I mean? The ones who can never seem to give you a straight answer or appear to go out of their way to create difficulties where there are none. Someone you just dread speaking to or seeing because you know what to expect and know beforehand that it will not be a pleasant experience. They will never change because that is just who they are. The one thing they excel at, however, is making the rest of realise that we do not want to be like them in any way, shape, or form. So, they have got one thing going for them, the only thing, but it is something.

June 4

"I aspire to inspire before I expire."
~ Pravinee Hurbungs

Catchy this one, isn't it? Short but very pertinent and apt! I do not think I am alone in hoping that when I do "expire" that, if I have not achieved absolutely everything I aspired to, it was not for the lack of trying. Also, hopefully along the way, I may have inspired at least one person (hopefully more) through my thoughts, words, or deeds, to live life to the full, pursue their dreams, always aim high, and never ever give up! What a legacy!

June 5

"Leave footprints of kindness wherever you go." ~ *Lori Deschene*

Isn't this a lovely quote? I really like this one, perhaps because it resonates with me personally as I do try to be kind to others, don't you? It costs us nothing but the smallest gesture of kindness, even just a smile, can mean more than we realise to the person on the receiving end. It is also amazing how people tend to hold onto a gesture or an act of kindness they have received and revisit it again and again when they feel the need just to know that people, for the most part, are kind. What do your footprints say?

June 6

"Sometimes those who challenge you most…. teach you the best." ~ *Unknown*

I can honestly say that hand on heart, I have met some really challenging people over the years. I will not bore you with the details, as I expect you have all got your own stories you could share too but, suffice to say, they have taught me valuable lessons. I know I did not think so at the time, and it was only later, usually much, much later, that I realised that I came out of the experience better equipped to deal with future challenging people. So, thank you, all you people who have challenged me in the past, thank you all very much indeed!

❈

June 7

"Our attitude toward life determines life's attitude towards us." ~ *John N. Mitchell*

Well, this does make sense don't you think? If we live life feeling positive, hopeful, and confident in our ability to cope, achieve and succeed, wouldn't it follow that this would pave the way for life to respond in kind? I believe it would be more likely than being pessimistic, doubting our abilities and having a "poor me" attitude towards other people and life in general. I know which one I would rather be don't you? So, what are you waiting for, if you are not already being optimistic, then make today the first day of your new outlook and see what happens…… I guarantee you will not regret it.

June 8

"I am not what happened to me. I am what I choose to become." ~ *Carl Jung*

Our experiences of and in life are what shape and mould us into the people we become. However, we too have a hand in shaping the malleable clay we represent when we are thrown on the spinning wheel of life in birthing what we will become. Then, it is how we respond to the people and events we encounter in life that shapes that further shapes us. Using the tools, we each have, i.e., free will, determination, confidence, the will to succeed and overcome, and more, which aids us in ultimately controlling who WE choose to be!

June 9

"Procrastination is the thief of time."
~ Edward Young

I am guilty of being a procrastinator! If procrastinating includes not being able to make a decision, then I am your woman. "Would you like a biscuit with your coffee" throws me into a panic? Should I think of my gradually expanding figure and refuse? Would I appear rude? Even if it is a biscuit I don't like (very unlikely but you never know)? I guess what this really means is that to procrastinate is to hesitate, and time spent hesitating means less time actually "doing" so time lost. We need to aim to be more decisive in acting sooner rather than later to thwart the thief, which is procrastination.

June 10

**"Take pride in how far you have come and
have faith in how far you can go."
~ *Christian Larson***

*We all doubt ourselves and our abilities at one
time or another, maybe more times than we can
count. However, this is normal so nothing to be
ashamed of. The thing to remember is that, while
it is healthy to doubt ourselves as it gives us an
opportunity to stop and think about what we are
doing and adjust things if we have to, it also pays
us to be more ready to give ourselves a pat on the
back. We all tend to be harder on ourselves than
anybody else would be, so take time to recognise
how far YOU have come and what YOU have
achieved and what you know YOU can achieve in
the future. Be kind to yourself, you are so worth it.*

June 11

"Defeat is a state of mind. No one is ever defeated until defeat has been accepted as a reality." ~ *Bruce Lee*

This is so true isn't it and makes perfect sense when you think about it. To be defeated by someone, an event or situation in our life, we would have to accept this without doubting for a single second that we had indeed lost the battle. Allowing this to become a reality in the experiences we file away in our brain would give it the power to negatively affect how we perceive ourselves from then on. Now why would we permit that to happen? Nope! We may have lost a minor skirmish, but we still have the ability to win the war and, by replacing that negativity with this positivity, gives our bruised and battered psyche the medicine it needs to heal and become whole again.

June 12

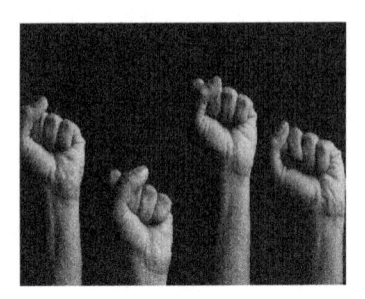

"The positive thinker Sees the invisible, Feels the Intangible, and Achieves the impossible." ~ *Winston Churchill*

Every one of us has the freedom to choose to think positively. How great is that? A gift to ourselves from ourselves. This benefit enables us to see the positive in the people around us, the situations we find ourselves in and the problems that we all face every day. How much better to arm ourselves with positivity rather than negativity to continue our path through life.

June 13

"Be the kind of person you want in your life."
~ Unknown

This brings to mind the saying, "Treat other people the way you would like to be treated" doesn't it? Do you live your life along these lines? I would like to believe that this is something I can relate to in my life and the lives of those closest to me. I like to believe the majority of us try to be the best we can be in our behaviour towards others, not just to those closest to us, but those we come across momentarily every day. Why wouldn't we?

June 14

"The quieter you become, the more you can hear." ~ *Ram Dass*

The world seems to get noisier every day, or is that just me? Cars driving past with their windows down and music blasting out so we can all get the "benefit" of the driver's musical predilections whether we want to or not, (usually not)! On a bus, coach or train, people continue conversations on their mobile 'phones. I would not mind so much if they were interesting with tasty bits of gossip but, often, they are boring to their fellow travellers. Do not get me started with headphones in public! Why can't people be content just to shhhhhh and be quiet. Don't they realise what they are missing? They might be pleasantly surprised at what they can hear, i.e., the sounds of the birds, children laughing, or squabbling, people having a pleasant conversation or, better still, only blessed silence.

June 15

"Once you awaken, you will have no interest in judging those who sleep."
~ *James Blanchard Cisneros*

I take this to mean a personal Spiritual awakening. A realisation that we are all Spiritually gifted and linked to each other just by being human beings. Personally, it took me a long time to become aware of my gifts and even longer to feel confident enough to use them in working professionally. Along the way I became aware that some of those not awakened Spiritually tended to dismiss or negatively treat anything to do with Spirituality. However, I am happy to leave those content to sleep to their slumbers without judgement.

June 16

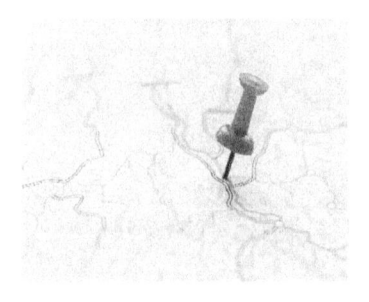

What lies behind us and what lies before us are tiny matters compared to what lies within us." ~ *Ralph Waldo Emerson*

Makes perfect sense, doesn't it? We all have a past, and many of us have a past that contains memories of things we have done or had done to us of which we would rather not be reminded. We are also ignorant of what the future holds for each one of us, but we all contain hope that it will contain happiness, prosperity, love etc. However, the one thing that is constant in all of this is US! We are the "ship" that is sailing the sea of life. We are the vessel continually taking aboard what we pick up on our voyage. Hopefully, we realise and learn as we journey what is good for us and what is not so good for us. However, the main lesson to learn here is that WE ourselves carry our past with us and will also absorb the future as we experience it so live in the moment and just BE!

June 17

"Though no one can go back and make a brand-new start, anyone can start from now and make a brand-new end." ~ *Unknown*

Like most of us, I occasionally look back and wish I could change some of the things that happened in my past, but I am realistic enough to know this will never be possible. However, what all of us can do is decide that, from now on, things are going to be different..." I am going to be different." Even if it is only changing your perception of someone or something it's a start and who knows where it will lead.... somewhere better than your previous thoughts were taking you that's for sure!

June 18

"We all cling to the past and, because we cling to the past, we become unavailable to the present." ~ *Bagwan Shree Rajneesh*

I do not agree that we all cling to the past, but I do believe that some of us tend to allow the past to dominate and affect our present. As a result, we are preventing ourselves from living life to the fullest at the present time and where does that get us? Stuck, that's where! We cannot go back, as what's done is done, and we're not moving forward if we are continually reliving the past so up to us to realise this and release the past, "bye, bye past and good riddance!" Now, bring it on........

June 19

"When something bad happens you have three choices, you can either let it define you, let it destroy you, or you can let it strengthen you." ~ *Dr. Seuss*

We don't have any control about the bad things that happen to us all at times on our journey in life, but we do have a choice as to how we deal with them. We can wear it like a cloak for everyone to see, allow it to overcome us and bring us to our knees or deal with it and move on. I know which one I would choose and it's not either of the first two choices. What would you choose?

June 20

"Things turn out best for the people who make the best of the way things turn out."
~ *John Wooden*

Exactly! I could not have said it better myself. We all know people who, when problematic situations, hard financial times, or personal strife happen to them, sail through whatever it is and come out the other end better than they went in! Unlike us, who when things like that happen to us, boy do we suffer! However, maybe they tackle what comes at them in a unique way. Perhaps, just by thinking positively, they already have a head start over the rest of us in overcoming whatever life throws at them. Maybe we should all try this for ourselves and see how we get on.

June 21

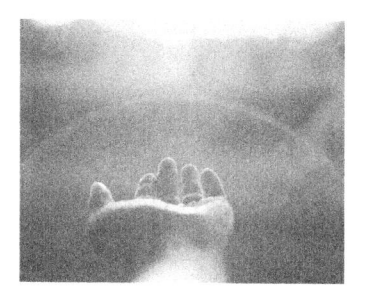

"It is during our darkest moments that we must focus to see the light."
~ *Aristotle Onassis*

The image this bring to my mind is of a miner's lamp! Do you know what I mean, the lamp they have on their helmets so they can see in the darkness of the tunnels they work in? In life, there will be times when all of us encounter darkness, totally devoid of any welcoming light, and very scary indeed. However, by focussing and believing in the light, we can turn a tiny, tiny glimmer of light into a light bright enough to banish all the darkness and shadows surrounding us. Remember, this will take total belief and focus, but we are all capable of achieving this, so the next time the darkness begins to close in, you know what you have to do, don't you?

June 22

"Forgive people who do you wrong…. they unknowingly make you strong."
~ *Mandy Hale*

Although we will not be thinking along these lines while people are or have done us wrong, this is actually absolutely true. Later, thinking about it, we begin to realise that, in having to cope with what they put us through, we do grow stronger. This could also help us cope better with the same or similar situations that confront us in the future, who would have thought it eh?

June 23

**"When you reach the end of your rope....
tie a knot in it and hang on."**
~ Franklin D. Roosevelt

Well, it makes more sense than no knot and just sliding off the end of your rope down into who knows what? Ooooh scary! I know I have often reached the end of my personal "rope" or ability to cope or deal with a situation or someone causing me stress or upset, and I am sure you have too. What do we do when we reach the end of our rope? Say, "That's it! I have had enough. I cannot deal with this anymore?" However, it is not going anywhere, is it? So, nothing else for it really but to "tie a knot in it" and hang on in there for dear life, until we consider it resolved and consign it to the bin of "past life resolutions" forever.

June 24

"Life is a great big canvas….and you should throw all the paint on it you can."
~ Danny Kaye

You can picture this, can't you? Imagine we all begin life as a huge, completely blank canvas and, as we move through life, our experiences, good and bad, positive, and not so positive, become the paint that colour our canvas. Wouldn't that be something to see? Would your own personal canvas be dominated by the dark dreary colours of disappointments, sadness, unfulfillment and lost opportunities, or the bright, vibrant colours of love, happiness, contentment, and achievement? I know which one I am working on day by day and hope you do too?

June 25

"Those who are unaware they are walking in darkness will never seek the light."
~ Bruce Lee

Well, why would they? If they are unaware that they are, in fact, surrounded by darkness they would have no reason to actively seek out the light, would they? Perhaps ignorance is bliss in this case? However, those of us fortunate enough to, not only have successfully sought out the light, but remain within its radiance, are truly fortunate indeed. Perhaps if we make our light accessible to all, more people will be drawn into this light and become as enlightened as we are... how wonderful would that be?

June 26

"Your life is your message to the World…. make it inspiring." ~ *Lorrin L. Lee*

A great many of us are usually so busy just dealing with our day-to-day lives that we never give a thought to how others truly see us, or the impact our lives may have on theirs. Stopping to think about how we do want other people to perceive us may give us pause to reflect on how we present ourselves. We should be giving our all every day to be the best and do the best we can as an example to all those who look to us for guidance and support. How great would that feel, to know that others may gain inspiration and purpose just by our example?

June 27

"Shoot for the moon. Even if you miss you'll land among the stars." ~ *Les Brown*

Go for it!! Whatever motivates you to do the best you can at what you love then harness that! Use it to keep your aim true and, if you're unsuccessful in reaching your own personal "moon," then finding yourself surrounded by the beautiful inspiring illumination of the stars wouldn't be too much of a disappointment, would it? Perhaps it's also where you were meant to land in the first place, who knows?

June 28

Every time I thought I was being rejected from something good, I was actually being re-directed to something better."
~ *Steve Maraboli*

I have lost count of the number of times this has been true for me, and I am sure, if you take the time to think back, that you can relate to this too. The job that was so meant for us that we did not get, the love interest that broke our heart, the planned holiday that did not materialise…on, and on, and on. Take another look at when this happened to you and think how different things would have been if they had happened as you had wanted and planned. I will wager that things did turn out well for you and that you may even have given a silent prayer of thanks as you were re-directed to something or someone much, much better. So, the next time you begin to rail against Fate when you did not get what you wanted, think about this, and wait and see….

June 29

"Some people FEEL the rain…others just get wet." ~ *Bob Marley*

Why do people moan and complain when it rains? Their ignorance really annoys me! Rain is life-sustaining, not only for us as human beings, but for our beautiful planet. Without it, every one of us would perish. Therefore, when it does rain I, for one, am truly thankful and do my utmost to enjoy being out in it, just to feel it on my skin, and see it do its job in nourishing our lives and all that surrounds us on our beautiful planet. Try to remember this the next time it rains and add your gratitude to mine.

June 30

"The only thing certain is…. nothing is certain." ~ *Michel De Montaigne*

You can certainly say that again! There is only one certainty in life and that's death. Apart from that, everything is by chance. We may think we have put certain things in place, at certain times, in certain locations, times, dates etc. However, as the saying goes, "Nothing is set in stone." There will always be the risk of plans going awry no matter how much time and effort you have put in to ensure this does not happen. Nothing we can do about it but just make our plans as we have always done and hope for the best, certain in the knowledge that nothing is certain!

July

July 1

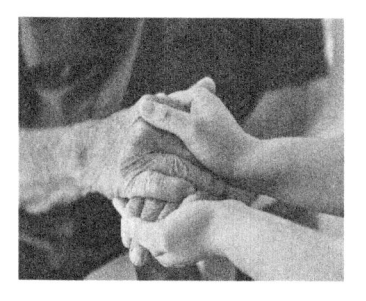

"Be kind wherever possible. It is always possible." ~ *Dalai Lama*

Now do I really have to explain or elaborate on this one? Thought not! There is absolutely no reason whatsoever for not being kind. We are all capable of bestowing kindness. It does not take any special skill or ability. It need not cost us anything, unless being kind in a particular situation, means spending a little too. If you take time to think about it, there is never ever a time when kindness is not possible unless you yourself decide not to be kind! But, then again, why wouldn't you? Of course, you wouldn't.... would you?

July 2

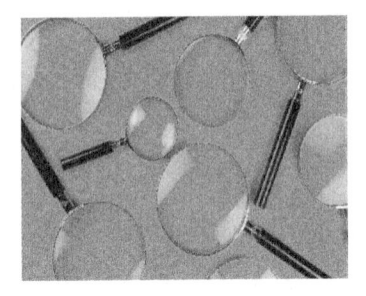

"Some things have to be believed to be seen." ~ *Ralph Hodgson*

Belief is something wonderful we are able to gift ourselves. When we genuinely believe, it is as if a veil has been removed from our eyes and we are able to see more clearly. However, it is up to each and every one of us to realise there is a veil there in the first place and then work to remove it or brush it aside. This also gives us the ability to "see" only with our mind's eye, the wonderful, magical, and inspiring people or places in Spirit form we would never be able to see with the naked eye.

July 3

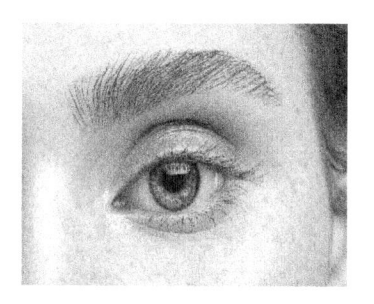

"We do not see things as they are. We see them as we are." ~ *Anais Nin*

Everything or everybody we see is "coloured" by our own personal perceptions based on what we have learned through time. That is just the way it is so there is nothing we can do about it, right? Wrong! If we are fortunate in being aware enough to realise this is what we are doing, we can take steps to change our thought process. See things from another's point of view. Be more considerate and weigh things up before deciding to pass judgement. As I said, that is just the way we are all shaped and coloured by life, so it is no bad thing, just something to be aware of for the future.

July 4

"Quiet people have the loudest minds."
~ Stephen James Smith

Often, we fail to notice people because they do their utmost to remain in the shadows or the fringes of our society. Looking on rather than participating in what's going on around them. However, just because they are quiet and keep themselves to themselves doesn't mean that their minds aren't working. In fact, they are probably doing a lot more thinking than the rest of us who are too busy with our interests and perhaps making our opinions known to anybody who will listen whether they want to or not. They take the time to really think and ponder so that, when they do have something to say, it may be a new innovative idea, the solution to an ongoing problem, or a profound statement. Never underestimate the quiet people in our midst but rather pay attention when they do have something to share with the rest of us, we might be pleasantly surprised.

July 5

"It is our choices that show what we truly are, far more than our abilities."
~ J.K. Rowling

We can be extremely talented and skilled at what we choose to do in life and may even be respected and admired because of it! However, rightly, or wrongly, other people judge us by the company we keep, the words we utter, and how we conduct ourselves in private and in public. They do this for the simple reason that these tend to truly reflect the choices WE make and, in turn, show us for who we really are. Therefore, wouldn't it be to our advantage to put thought and care into these choices? I know I do.

July 6

"Whatever you are willing to put up with is exactly what you will have." ~ *Unknown*

This is down to individual choice, isn't it? We choose who and what we allow into our life, so it follows that we know what we are getting into right? If only it were that simple? Sometimes the choices we make begin very promisingly and everything in the garden is rosy so to speak and we are happy. However, perhaps some distance down the line, things do not stay rosy and turn into something vastly different. This is where we must make a choice. We either stay in the situation as it is, aware nothing will change for the better, or we choose to leave. If we do stay, fully aware of the latter, then the consequences are on our own head. I know what I would choose…what about you?

July 7

"You were born an original. Don't die a copy." ~ *John Mason*

Isn't that a wonderful thought? We are all, every one of us, born an original? Each unique in our own way which will continue until the day we pass to Spirit. Each of us absorbing and experiencing whatever life has in store for us, no two lives exactly the same. When you consider the population of planet Earth, that's quite a thought isn't it? However, some people, for reasons of their own, strive to emulate someone else, usually a film star or a usually short-lived pop sensation, or just someone they know personally and admire. Not me! Nor you either, I hope? Be the unique being you are when passing from this world as you were coming into it. Easy peasy!

July 8

"The pen that writes your life story must be held in your own hand." ~ *Irene C. Kassorla*

Of course, it must! Common sense really. Otherwise, it would be like allowing somebody else to do your job, meet and marry your spouse, have your children.... Make the choices assuring the most beneficial outcome for you. Experience what you choose to. Do not be pressured by anyone else into doing anything you do not want to. Do not allow anybody to dictate your life story. The clue is in the "your." Remember that okay?

July 9

"The human Spirit needs places where nature has not been rearranged by the hand of man." ~ *Unknown*

This really resonates with me on a personal level. When I find that I am beginning to feel overloaded with whatever is going on in my life, the only thing that never fails to invigorate and restore me is either a nice amble in the countryside or, even better, time spent at the seashore. Fortunately, we live only a 10-minute walk away from the sea so how great is that? I believe that nothing can restore the human Spirit more than spending time in the great outdoors, away from houses, cars, crowds, etc. Our Spirit thrives on being "free" from the restraints of modern life and takes on new life and vigour from being allowed to commune with the very basics necessary to sustain life.

❦

July 10

"Spirituality is a personal relationship with the Divine. Religion is crowd control."
~ Unknown

I only came across this quote recently and I must admit it did strike a chord. It really made me think more deeply about Spirituality and Religion. I have always believed that there is "something," a higher power if you like, that inspires and challenges us all. However, I also passionately believe that we are all entitled to our own individual, personal beliefs, which should be respected by everybody who knows us. To me that is Spirituality. On the other hand, I have found a few Religions to be the result of somebody else's interpretation of how we should behave and think and does not tolerate (however much it professes to) any deviation from its teaching. I dislike the hypocrisy involved. This is my personal opinion. However, I also respect the rights of others in being entitled and allowed to follow their own beliefs and hope you agree?

July 11

"If you propose to speak, always ask yourself, is it true, is it necessary, is it kind?" ~ *Rev. James Haldane Stewart*

We are all guilty, at one time or another, of speaking or commenting without firstly engaging our brain first, aren't we? I am sure I am not alone in this. It would really serve us well to think carefully before allowing what is in our head to pass through our lips because once it is said, it cannot be unsaid. No matter how much you protest and try to explain you did not mean it, it came out all wrong, they have taken it the wrong way, etc. etc., it is out there and could have consequences or repercussions that may reverberate down the tunnel of time. So, my friends, the next time you are tempted to let it "all out," ask yourself the above three questions first.... If the answer is no, keep it zipped so to speak or rather, do not speak!

July 12

"Nothing is stronger than habit."
~ Theodore Roosevelt

One of the best habits you could ever develop is to get into the habit of being thankful and grateful for the people and things in your life. It's sometimes oh so easy to get into the habit of seeing the "cup half empty" rather than the "cup half full." We all have habits, whether we realise it or not, and a habit can be a strength so use your habits to enhance how you look at life and count your blessings rather than nurture habits that detract from the quality of the life you believe you're leading. Doesn't this make sense?

July 13

"Change your thoughts and you change your world." ~ Norman Vincent Peale

Not something that ever occurred to me before I came across this quote but, when I did, it made perfect sense. It is only natural that as we grow and mature into the person we are destined to become that our thoughts grow with us. We subconsciously allow our thoughts to shape us in what we come to believe and how we perceive the people or events we encounter on our journey through life. These thoughts become "who we are" and I, for one, never took the time to examine and explore just who I "am." However, fortunately, for the past several years I have changed my thought pattern, around what I am capable of achieving and what kind of person I want to be. Taking time to do this changed my whole perception of my world. Time for some thought spring cleaning in your life....?

July 14

"The measure of who we are is what we do with what we have." ~ *Vince Lombardi*

So simple, so true! I believe that we all begin life with the ability to achieve. Unfortunately, some of us are born into circumstances of poverty, careless or cruel parenting, handicapped in some way etc., therefore opportunities to achieve, if any, may be few and far between. That which defines us is not where we begin but where we end. If we use whatever we have, even if it is the single ability to overcome and endure, then that's wonderful. We are using what no one can take from us, because it is within us, ours to hold and nurture. We are all, every one of us, incredibly special indeed.

July 15

"If opportunity doesn't knock, build a door." ~ *Milton Berle*

Now doesn't that just make perfect sense? I am a great believer in that adage, "If you don't ask, you don't get" so, if there is something I want to do, and I need someone else's agreement, I ask! If I get rejected, at least I am not always going to regret not asking and wondering about the outcome for a long time to come. If I get the green light, well done me for asking. That's the "door." Always be prepared to "knock" and ask and you just might be pleasantly surprised. What have you got to lose?

July 16

"Keep your face always toward the sunshine – and shadows will fall behind you." ~ *Walt Whitman*

Easy to say but not so easy to do! We have all had times and, no doubt, will again, when we have felt the sun would never shine again for us. Times when perhaps life has pulled on boxing gloves, and we have been defenceless against the ensuing onslaught. Some blows can be dodged or parried so they land lightly and, although painful, we can recover quickly. However, some blows may knock the very breath from us and bring us to our knees, defeated. However, we all have the spark of endurance, of living to fight another day within us so use this to lift your face to the sun and banish the shadows to the past where they belong.

July 17

"Your big opportunity may be right where you are now." ~ *Napoleon Hill*

We all tend to be always looking ahead, dreaming of that big break, the opportunity of a lifetime, and everything falling into place just the way we have always imagined it. However, what is to say that our big opportunity isn't within our grasp right now, today, this minute? Spending all our time thinking about the future may prevent us from appreciating the here and now, when what we have always dreamed of is right under our nose, impatient to be manifested. So, continue to dream and while envisaging what you so desperately want but, occasionally, just take the time to stop and consider what is happening around you NOW! Your big opportunity could be right under your nose!

July 18

"The best preparation for tomorrow is doing your best today."
~ *H. Jackson Brown Junior*

Well, this is only common sense, isn't it? If we do our best today, in everything we do, and behave our best towards everybody we encounter in our day, then we will have peace of mind won't we? Realistically, this will be easier to achieve on some days than others as we are not saints but human beings. However, if we can lay our head on our pillow at bedtime and, looking back on our day, be happy and content with how it has gone and how we have conducted ourselves, then tomorrow is like cash in the bank, another day to look forward to, zzzz...

July 19

"You are always free to change your mind and choose a different future, or a different past." ~ *Richard Bach*

I was not sure what this meant at first. I could relate to choosing a different future but a different past, really? I believe you are NEVER too old to choose a different future to the one you envisaged when you were much younger. Life tends to change and shape us in ways we never expected or planned for. There is nothing stopping us responding to these changes by adapting and putting into practice new plans or ideas. However, when it comes to choosing a different past... I do not think this is so much about choosing a different past but instead learning from the past and allowing the lessons it has taught us to enhance our future. This is our choice, so we need to use it wisely.

July 20

"The most wasted of all days is one without laughter." ~ *E.E. Cummings*

I can really relate to this. I love a good laugh. I don't know anybody who doesn't, and I do not suppose you do either? I agree with the well-known saying that laughter is the best medicine. There have been scientific studies that prove that laughter can be greatly beneficial to people suffering from physical or mental illness. I know it works for me if I am having a difficult day when things appear to be conspiring to make my day one where I just want to go to bed and hide under the duvet. Being able to find humour in any situation is not easy but it pays us to really try, as things tend to not seem so bad if we can don't you think?

July 21

"When you do what you fear most, then you can do anything." ~ *Stephen Richards*

Fear makes us prisoners of us. It prevents us from doing the things we want to, even preventing our dreams from becoming reality, because we ourselves allow it power over us. Why not give it a "bloody nose" by taking your power back? Go on, gather all your courage, believe in YOU, and do what you fear the most. You will find that nothing terrible happened but that you feel great and experience a wonderful sense of "release" because that old bogeyman "Fear" has been banished forever. YOU have given yourself the great gift of a fear-free life apart, of course, when fear works in your favour and prevents you from doing something dangerous, then it's ok!

July 22

**"To dream by night is to escape your life.
To dream by day is to make it happen."
~ *Stephen Richards***

I usually have very vivid dreams. You know the kind that, when you wake up, you can remember not all of it, but certain bits and don't they feel real? I have given up trying to find meanings in most of them although some are obviously born from what I have read or watched on TV previously. In fact, when I think about it, dreams are like programmes appearing on the screen of our sleeping mind. We are at the mercy of our very own, personal, unique show. On the other hand, our daytime dreams can only play out for us if WE take the time, energy, and commitment to make them reality. We are the Producers and Directors solely responsible for bringing our dreams into being. Scene 1 ....

July 23

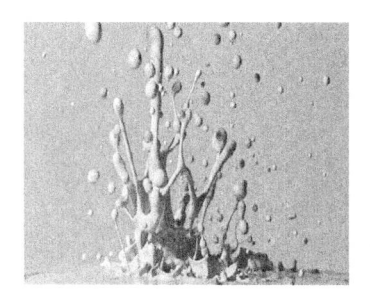

"You are not a drop in the ocean, you are an entire ocean in a drop." ~ *Rumi*

I know there are times when I feel insignificant, perhaps due to unforeseen events or the actions or words of other people. I guess we all do at one time or another. That we do not matter or figure in the grand scheme of things and that everybody else on the planet does. Sound familiar? I thought so. However, try looking at yourself another way. YOU are a vessel filled with dreams, hope, energy, feelings, etc., all crammed into one unique human being. There is NOBODY else like YOU on the entire planet! You are a unique being. A "one off" among men (and women!). How great is that? How reassuring! Try remembering this the next time you begin to feel insignificant. YOU? Insignificant? Really? Never!!

July 24

"Forgiveness is the attribute of the strong."
~ Mathatma Gandhi

See, this is something I am not totally convinced of to be honest. Let me think.... Okay, so if you hold onto your anger, your grudge, your dissatisfaction, how will this make you weak? Perhaps by totally occupying your mind to the exclusion of anything else, and by tainting your whole outlook on life and people in general from that day forward. So, who is going to suffer most from this? Well, you yourself, of course. By holding on tightly to something that is not doing you any favours will obviously prevent you from being free of bitterness and consequently enjoying and living your life fully. So, to be strong, you need to forgive and, by the conscious act of forgiveness, allow yourself the freedom to pursue a happy, peaceful life. Oh, I get it now! Do you?

July 25

"Every Saint has a past, and every Sinner has a future." ~ *Oscar Wilde*

I always think of a Saint, as someone just like you or me who has triumphed over many disasters, obstacles, and difficulties in his/her life, while still having faith in humankind and finding joy in life. Perhaps, the means they have used to overcome and succeed are better forgotten as they may not have been the most honourable or fair. However, if they now live their lives respectably, are considerate towards their fellow humans and are being the best they can be, then who are we to judge? The same applies to a "sinner." Someone who acknowledges their past sins or transgressions and resolves to be a better person in the future, in my eyes at least, deserves all the support and encouragement we can offer them.

July 26

"I close my eyes in order to see."
~ Paul Gauguin

Sometimes, just sometimes, this is incredibly good advice. Occasionally, when you find yourselves going over and over a tricky situation, or a problem you are experiencing, it would pay you to just close your eyes. Close your eyes and settle your mind. Not easy initially but persevere, it will be worth it. Now, calming all your senses, try thinking about what is troubling you. Without any visual stimulation or any distractions, you may find it easier to think more clearly and, hopefully, find the answer you need or a way to resolve a troubling situation more easily.

July 27

"Love…. if you don't have it, no matter what else you may have, it's not enough."
~ Ann Landers

I could not agree more! Those who are not fortunate enough to have love in their life spend all their time and energy searching for it. Although, according to most of what we read online, in popular magazines or publications, we are all striving to look young, beautiful, thin, and rich, in no particular order. Yeah right! Anybody possessing at least one functioning brain cell knows that if you have at least one person in the world who loves you, or indeed you just love yourself, unconditionally, then you have it all. Sure, it helps if you have a roof over your head, food in your stomach and enough money to pay your way in life, but love is like the icing on the cake and what a cake!

July 28

"Go out looking for one thing and that's all you'll ever find." ~ *Robert J. Flaherty*

This reminds me of horses with their blinkers on, unable to see anything but what is straight ahead. They do not have a choice about whether to be blinkered but we do, don't we? If we choose not to see the opportunities and possibilities "outside the box" then we have only ourselves to blame. We should strive to be open to every opportunity that comes our way in life. We do not need to take each one presented to us, but we should at least acknowledge it as an opportunity, consider it, and either discard it or go for it! Who knows what adventures we will have and the treasure we will discover? Wonderful!

July 29

**"To be alive, to be able to see, to walk....
it's all a miracle." ~ *Arthur Rubenstein***

I must admit I have been guilty, many times in my life, of having taken for granted the blessings I have, in just being able to see, hear, walk, touch etc. It is so easy sometimes just to feel sorry for ourselves over something trivial. Perhaps bemoaning the fact that we do not have as much money as we would like, or are as successful as we had hoped, etc. etc. It isn't until we read something in a newspaper, hear a comment on the radio, or view a programme on the television, about an individual or a group of people who can't see, hear, walk or are suffering some catastrophe or hardship, that we realise that actually, you know what, we are truly blessed with the gifts we have and should take the time more often just to give thanks for what we do have. I do now.

July 30

"True religion is the life we lead, not the creed we profess." ~ *Louis Nizer*

Need I say more? I have witnessed people who attend Church faithfully every Sunday and profess themselves Christians be guilty of "casting the first stone" or never practising what they preach. I especially dislike the riches and treasures some religions seem to consider their "due," while their followers are rife with disease because they cannot afford medicines, starving because of a lack of food, have no roof over their heads or no clean drinking water etc. What is that all about? Personally, I think it is obscene and it really saddens me, as I guess it does you. I try to live my life being the best I can be and treating others the way I would like to be treated. It works for me. What about you? Can you relate to this?

July 31

"The door you open to give love, is the very one through which love arrives."
~ Alan Cohen

Lovely, isn't it? Makes sense too. If we keep ourselves closed off from allowing love access, i.e., keeping our own personal "door to love" firmly shut, then how is love ever going to gain entry? It is obviously not is it and, let's face it, we all need love in our lives. Love is like the rain that falls and nourishes the earth and everything that grows upon it. It encourages us all to reach for our own personal sunshine and bask in the knowledge that we love and are loved in return. I believe the world would be a much better place if only every single one of us determined to encourage love to flourish and propagate.

August

234

August 1

"New beginnings are often disguised as painful endings." ~ *Lao Tzu*

This could apply to a relationship, a job, a home, a belief, anything that causes us pain emotionally because it is ending. This may be the result of a choice we have made or a decision by someone else. Although we may not realise it at the time because we are still feeling the pain of our loss, this could have left us free to pursue a brand new, exciting, fruitful new beginning. An opportune time to welcome in new opportunities, to realise new dreams, even just to enjoy a newfound freedom. So, before mourning an ending, try to welcome the new beginnings on offer just for you.

August 2

"If you want to go fast, go alone. If you want to go far, go together."
~ African Proverb

Two options offered here. Your decision as to which one is for you. Both have their advantages and disadvantages, just like everything in life. If you want to get where you want to go as quickly as possible, with no thought for anybody or anything else, then best not to feel hampered by too much "baggage" which could slow or impede your progress. However, when you get to the finishing post, you may be disappointed nobody there waits there to applaud your efforts or share in your achievement. If, however, you choose companions to offer support and encouragement as you travel, this may work to your advantage as two heads, or more, tend to work better than one. Which option would you choose?

August 3

"Accept what is, let go of what was, and have faith in what will be." ~ *Sonia Ricotti*

There will be times in all our lives when we will feel unfairly done by. I am sure it is nothing personal on the part of the Universe, just how things are. It is up to us, as individuals, to learn and to accept these lessons, because that's just what they are meant to be for us, something to experience and learn from. The trick is to acknowledge, learn, accept, and trust. Trust that we have taken on board what we need to be aware of at a particular time in our life and accepting that what will be will be for our benefit in the future.

August 4

"Wealth consists not in having great possessions, but in having few wants."
~ Epictetus

This is the type of wealth worth having. Sure, monetary wealth is great, and we could not exist without it, but "true" wealth is another story. These are the riches we possess by having the people we love and who love us close by, our health and the health of those we love, the ability to laugh, experience happiness, cry tears of joy, have enough money to pay our way through life without counting every penny. The list is endless, but you know what I mean? If we have all that and more, what else could possibly be found wanting in our lives...?

August 5

"Storms make trees take deeper roots."
~ Dolly Parton

I guess Dolly means this is because the rain unleashed by a storm soaks into the earth, nourishing the roots and enabling them to grow even stronger and deeper. Compare this to us as human beings. The "storms" that we experience are portrayed by the trials and tribulations of everyday life and the "rain" as how we deal with them. By allowing ourselves to absorb and learn from what we are experiencing, we nourish our ability to gain strength to make us even stronger so that the next time a "storm" strikes we are more prepared to deal with it thanks to our "roots."

August 6

**"The most important thing in
communication is to hear what isn't said."
~ *Peter F. Drucker***

I know this sounds a bit strange but, if you think about it, it does make sense. How many times have you said something to someone because it is what you know they want to hear but not really what you wanted to say? The same could also apply to comments or remarks to you from someone else. However, I believe we are also astute when it comes to knowing when something is not being said, either due to consideration of our feelings or because they do not feel they have the right words to convey what they mean or feel. Sometimes, it is better to say nothing at all rather than say the wrong thing at the wrong time.

❁

August 7

"The only person you are destined to become is the person you decide to be."
~ Ralph Waldo Emerson

Exactly! So, what is stopping you from deciding exactly who you want to be? Do not allow it to be you yourself, will you? This is in YOUR hands and within YOUR power so decide wisely. Choose your path and the tools you need to carve out and mould the person you ultimately see yourself as being with careful consideration. Do not rush any part of the work you put in. What a masterpiece you are going to be. I look forward to your unveiling.

August 8

"The gem cannot be polished without friction, nor man without trials."
~ *Confucius*

I do not know a great deal about the actual process of transforming a chunk of carbon into a diamond, but I do know that it takes a great deal of pressure and skill in shaping it into the precious gem it will become. The same applies to us. We are all exposed to pressure from various sources throughout life and, just like a diamond, how we react, cling to, or discard, these ultimately play a part in moulding us into the finished product we are in life. Let us hope that we all end up the precious stones we were meant to be!

August 9

**"Too many of us are not living our dreams
because we are living our fears."
~ *Les Brown***

Wouldn't it be a pity if we allowed our fear of failure, or the discouragement of others, to prevent us embarking on a path to make our dreams come true? However, I do realise that we are all different and it may be great deal more difficult for some of us to summon up the courage, focus and determination to pursue what we want most in life than others blessed with more "get up and go" and belief in themselves. It would therefore take more courage, more focus, and more determination for these people to achieve their dreams, but wouldn't the end result be doubly sweet?

August 10

"You often meet your destiny on the road you've taken to avoid it." ~ *Unknown*

I believe there is no side-stepping or avoiding destiny no matter how fancy your footwork! The clue is in the word! Your destiny is your destiny and that's that, no room for manouvering whatsoever. You may think you have outsmarted good ole destiny but, while giving yourself a congratulatory pat on the back, discover it is staring you in the face. Some things, a few good, a few not so good, are destined for us to encounter and deal with in life so best just to accept and get on with it. There is no alternative.

August 11

"There is no security in this life. There is only opportunity." ~ Douglas MacArthur

This is like saying there is no certainty in life so make the best of it, don't you think? Nothing is secure or lasts forever. Things change from second to second, from minute to minute, hour to hour. Do not let this ever prevent you from searching out and seizing every opportunity that you discover or that is presented to you. Find your own security in the knowledge that no opportunity has ever slipped through your grasp!

August 12

"Problems are not stop signs; they are guidelines." ~ *Robert H. Schuller*

When we are experiencing problems, we do not think of them as stop signs, oh no, we think of them as something we could really do without! Many problems result from our own actions, and some do not. However, whatever their origin they are problems just the same so need to be dealt with. Maybe we should look at our next problem as a guideline? By dealing with it and learning from it we will have a clearer understanding of how to deal with the same or similar problem the next time it rears its ugly head, so a lesson learned, right?

August 13

"What you do today can improve all your tomorrows." ~ *Ralph Marston*

Of course, it can! This can come about in so many ways. By studying for a decent job or career, meeting and committing to that special someone in your life, where you choose to live, friendships, in fact, the decisions you make every single day... I could go on and on, but you get my drift, don't you? Ensure you take enough time to weigh up and consider any possible negative or unfulfilling results of your decisions before choosing to make the next stage of your life a reality. It is all in your hands. The decisions and choices you make in and through your life will create the happiness and contentment of your tomorrows...or not, as the case may be...

August 14

"Always be a first-rate version of yourself, instead of a second-rate version of somebody else." ~ *Judy Garland*

Now why would you want to be somebody else in the first place? Saying that, just by being aware of all the magazines, TV programmes and advertising that bombard the younger among us, this seems to be the case. They actively encourage our younger generation to venerate the "celebrities" they promote. I am sure that, just like me, you see them for what most of them are, i.e., narcissistic, self-obsessed, vacuous, airheads, who regard a chipped or broken fingernail as a major crisis, and that is just the men! Seriously, we need to do our bit to ensure that the youngsters under our influence realise that they are incredibly special, unique individuals, who can accomplish wonderful things in life just by being who they were born to be.

August 15

"In order to succeed, we must first believe that we can." ~ *Nikos Kazantzakis.*

Well of course we must! This belief is what will motivate our will to succeed and ensure we persevere when the going gets tough as success, wherever we seek to achieve it, may prove worthless without struggle or self-sacrifice. Arming ourselves with the belief and determination that we WILL succeed in our chosen quest must be the first and most important lesson to learn. Once we have absorbed this way of thinking into our very being, then nothing or no one who attempts to stand in the way of our success will prevent us from reaching our personal goal, or goals!

August 16

"Life isn't about finding yourself. Life is about creating yourself."
~ *George Bernard Shaw*

Going by what I have read or come across recently in the media, there are a great many people professing to be attempting to find themselves. I find myself wondering when we can expect to see someone putting their hand up, in order to be noticed, while announcing "Hurray, I've found myself, aren't I clever?" Some unfortunate people may spend so much time trying to find themselves in life that, one day, reality sets in and they realise that there isn't any point anymore as their life is almost over. How sad! So, please don't let that be you, will you? Spend every single day of your life creating who you want to be, what you want to achieve, follow your dreams, and occasionally dare to take a step or two into the unknown. Don't you be that unfortunate soul looking back on life from old age and shedding tears of regret for what might have been.

August 17

"Life is really simple, but we insist on making it complicated." ~ *Confucius*

Oh, we do, don't we? However, I do not think it is all our fault but due to the time we are living in. We are faced with so many choices now about where to shop, what to eat, where to take the kids, schools, leisure activities, what to read. I could go on, but you get the gist, right? Okay, so what we need to do is consciously uncomplicate (is that even a word?) our own life when we can. Make a choice and stick to it. If there is something you can do to simplify the way you shop, work, or run your household, then do it. Simple!

August 18

"In the end, it's not the years in your life that count. It's the life in your years."
~ Abraham Lincoln

Definitely! I guess we all know young people who behave as if they were a lot older in the way they live their daily lives and their outlook on life. We consider them "old before their time" don't we? Such a pity. Then there are the not so young (me included) who have learned to enjoy every day no matter what it brings and celebrate just being alive and able to do most of the things we want to. The wise among us realise we should not allow age to restrict our joy in just being alive. Make plans to do what you enjoy doing most. Try to make new friends, start a new hobby or pastime. Make every day an adventure to be enjoyed and you will not go far wrong. Go on, what are you waiting for? Off you go!

August 19

"Positive thinking is better than negative nothing." ~ *Elbert Hubbard*

Personally, I have always been a great believer in positive thinking. It just makes perfect sense to me. What is the alternative? Always thinking negatively or fearing the worst prevents us from exploring and succeeding at the opportunities or relationships presented to us in life. Surely, it is more to our advantage to think "ok, I'm not too sure about this but I will give it a go and see what happens" than to be negative, opt out, and the opportunity is lost forever so you will never know what might have been? I would rather take the former option, what about you?

August 20

"Yesterday is not ours to recover, but tomorrow is ours to win or lose."
~ Lyndon B. Johnson

Aha, I get it! Once yesterday has gone it has gone right? It may not have been such a wonderful day for us so perhaps we are very relieved to see it go. Tomorrow, however, is another brand-new opportunity for us to make it a wonderful day by what we do and how we behave. Aren't we blessed to have a new day to look forward to? So let us respect this gift by our intention to do our utmost to make it a winning day, and the next day, and the next...

August 21

"Once you replace negative thoughts with positive ones, you'll start having positive results." ~ *Willie Nelson*

Of course, you will! Self-belief and determination to being optimistic will show that you can achieve the positive results you wish for in life. I passionately believe that it is important that what you put "out there" is positive as this is vital in creating the positive outcome for which you are aiming. Negativity has no place in this process so be sure to remember this and you will not go far wrong.

August 22

"Believe that life is worth living and your belief will help create the fact."
~ *William James*

Now why would you think otherwise? Of course, you wouldn't! Like me, you realise that we are extremely fortunate just to be alive and able to enjoy this wonderful world we inhabit. Because we are very blessed in being aware of this, we can indeed take steps to make this a reality, not only for us, but for everyone around us. However, unfortunately, not all of us are so fortunate or as aware. Therefore, it is up to us to give thanks for our own awareness and our ability to create the life we are living.

August 23

"We know what we are but know not what we may be." ~ *William Shakespeare*

This is one of the wonderful things about us human beings, our ability to achieve. We all know who we are and what we are capable of, and our own limitations. Wait a minute though! Have we ever stopped to think about the limitations we consciously, or subconsciously, place upon ourselves? Maybe it is about time we did. To help us manifest who we want to be determined to shake off those darned limitations and see what happens. Who is with me?

August 24

"In the middle of every difficulty lies opportunity." ~ *Albert Einstein*

I guess this very much depends on how we cope when confronted with a tricky situation. We may be unsuccessful in overcoming and resolving whatever confronts us. However, it need not be a total disaster if we learn from the lessons, it taught us. What worked and what did not? What, if anything, could we have done differently? Do not allow what you failed at on one occasion to prevent you from the opportunity it gave you to add to your problem-solving skills and move on, better equipped to succeed the next time life throws presents you with a challenge.

August 25

"If the wind will not serve, take to the oars." ~ *Latin Proverb*

Now, you know what this means don't you? Basically, if the "wind," i.e., your thoughts and ideas aren't getting you where you want to be, then you need to implement your "oars," i.e., physical action. You may have come to the realisation that the plans you have in your head will not materialise as you want them to unless you take the necessary steps to implement them. So, be grateful you have your own "oars" when the "wind" fails so that you will not be left drifting aimlessly but able to reach the destination YOU have chosen.

August 26

"Trust yourself. You know more than you think you do." ~ *Benjamin Spock*

Human nature can be guilty of letting us down occasionally. By that, I mean we can all tend to doubt ourselves and our abilities, or what we perceive to be our lack of abilities. The trick here is to trust that we know much, much more than we think we do. Lack of trust in ourselves does us no favours whatsoever, so why do we allow it this power over us? Exactly! I don't know either. So, let us agree that, from now on, we all strive to believe in our own powers, okay?

August 27

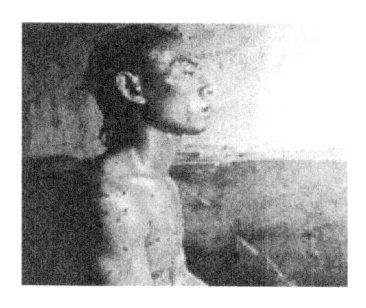

"Life is 10% what happens to me and 90% how I react to it." ~ *Charles R. Swindoll*

The 10% refers to the actual amount of control we personally have over what happens to us in life. It therefore follows that we are 90% at the mercy of influences we have no control over. This is just a tad disturbing don't you think? I expect, like me, you thought it would be more 50/50? However, it does makes sense. Imagine the 10% is a small stone or pebble that you toss into a deep, still pool of water. Watch as the ripples expand outwards, outwards, and outwards.... well, that's the other 90%. The 10% we initiate causes a reaction that may have far-reaching consequences, either favourable or not so favourable for us. The way we individually respond and react shapes us into the person we become in life. How do you think you have done so far?

August 28

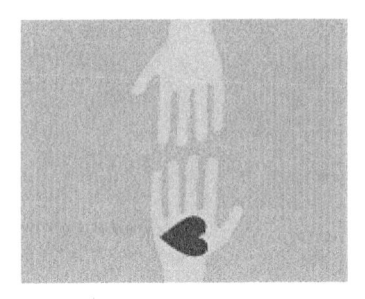

"I always wondered why somebody didn't do something about that; then I realised that I am that somebody." ~ *Lily Tomlin*

Sadly, I imagine that this strikes a chord, not only with me, but with you too. We read something awful in a newspaper, see a news report on TV, or witness something more personal and closer to home, and wonder why nobody is doing anything about it. Wouldn't it make more sense if we did not rely on someone else to take the action required, but instead did what was necessary ourselves? What do you think?

August 29

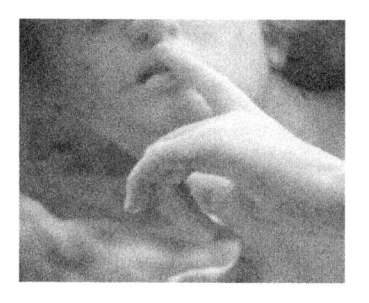

"Remember, no one can make you feel inferior without your consent."
~ Eleanor Roosevelt

Of course, they can't! You are a positive person, self-confident, sure of yourself and your many gifts and abilities so why would you allow anybody the power to make you feel inferior? You would not of course. Nobody has this right. So, commit to continuing as you mean to go on in the future, secure in the knowledge that you are as good as, if not better than, those who would seek to make you feel inferior. Click the belief switch and off you go. Well done you.

August 30

"If a man wants his dreams to come true, he must wake them up." ~ *Unknown*

To make your dreams come true it is a clever idea to have a dream in mind in the first place. Then, once you have decided on your dream, or dreams, it is down to you to do everything you can to make it or them a reality. Be careful not to get distracted and risk losing sight of your dream(s), as it is only through your focus, determination, and perseverance that they can be manifested into reality. Nourish, nurture, and ultimately reap the rewards. Then, onto the next dream as you're on a roll!

August 31

"If you do what you do well enough, long enough, consistently enough and fast enough, you will win the race."
~ Jessie Potter

*Being tenacious is the key to achieving, not just being first past the post, but actually getting as far as the post. We all know that life can throw us some hard knocks and setbacks along the way and sometimes feel it's so much easier just to throw in the towel and give up. However, by believing you can succeed and, indeed **will** succeed, and persevering again and again, perhaps in the face of fierce opposition, will see you triumph in the end through your own tenacity. What a boost for your self-esteem that is! See you at the winning post!*

September

September 1

"To live is the rarest thing in the world. Most people exist, that is all." ~ *Oscar Wilde*

Incredibly sad but absolutely true. Most people are so caught up in the day-to-day struggle just to earn a living that they are totally unaware of how fortunate they are just to be healthy and alive. Quick to rail against life when it deals them a blow or does not deliver what they want when they want it. However, those of us who are fortunate enough to realise how blessed we truly are just to be alive and able to truly "live" life to the full because of it, should view those who are not as lucky, with compassion. There but for the Grace of God............

September 2

"Don't compare or compete…. Be unique."
~ Unknown

We all start out totally unique but, as time passes, it is only natural that we absorb what is around us and sooner or later we may realise we are not as unique anymore, but just one of the crowd. It is never too late to change this if you really, really want to. Simple really, all you need to do is allow YOUR thoughts and ideas, YOUR beliefs, YOUR view of the world and the people in it, to guide you. By all means, read or view what you are being constantly bombarded with by the media, either in print or digitally. However, remain true to the kind of person you want to be not somebody else's idea of how you should look, what you should wear or eat, etc. That is not for you, because you are aware you are unique, right?

September 3

"If someone dumps on you…. use it as compost." ~ *Unknown*

Not a very pleasant turn of phrase but it does serve a purpose. There cannot be many of us who have not been "dumped" on by someone in the past. Totally unexpectedly, out of the blue, did not see that coming…. but dumped on, nevertheless. It is what we decide to do with what has been dumped on us that separates the men from the boys or the women from the girls. Use the "dump" as compost in your own personal virtual garden and see how the flowers named "lessons learned" grow tall and strong. Hopefully, that will be all the compost you will ever need.

September 4

"People with tact…. have less to retract."
~ Arnold H. Glasgow

Or, to put it another way, think before you speak. Unfortunately, this is not something everybody is able to put into practice and, personally, I have been guilty of putting my foot in it more than once. However, thankfully, through time, I have learned that if I take the time to ensure that what I am about to say will not cause offence to whoever is on the receiving end, then there is less chance of it coming back to "bite me on the bu…'er bottom!" So, please try to follow my example. Trust me, it will save you a great deal of back-pedaling in the future so well worth it.

September 5

"The best angle to approach any problem is the try-angle." ~ *Unknown*

Clever play on words don't you think? Makes a lot of sense too. If you have a problem surely the best and most efficient way to deal with it is to be prepared to tackle it head on! What is the alternative, pretend it's not there? It will not go away just because you are ignoring it! In fact, to get your full attention, it will stand in your path and make itself as big and nasty as it can, ooo 'er! So, don't you think that the very sensible thing to do would be to try and make it go away while it is still small enough not to be as scary as it could be if you continue to ignore it? This is where the "try" comes in and the clue is in the word! Next time a problem rears its ugly head, try it, and see.

September 6

"The older I get, the less I care about what people think of me. Therefore, the older I get, the more I enjoy life." ~ *Unknown*

Getting older does have its benefits which I consider wonderful in having the power to really set free. During most of my earlier life what other people thought of me really mattered and greatly influenced how I saw myself. However, with age comes a great many unexpected blessings, one of which is not giving a hoot what anybody else thinks of me. I love and enjoy my life just as it is and try to live it to the full. I also do and say what I please nowadays and if other people do not like it or agree with me well, I just do not care, so there!

September 7

"When nothing goes right…. Go left."
~ *Martha Cecilia*

This made me laugh while, at the same time, I wondered about the meaning. I guess it just tells us that, at those times when nothing appears to be going right for us, maybe we need to consider changing direction. I do believe that, if something we are trying to accomplish is beset by continual delays, problems, disappointments, then perhaps "something" is trying to tell us that we need to think again. So, going left or just in another direction from our original planned path, might prove more successful? Only time will tell if we have "got the message."

September 8

"Everything you need comes to you in perfect time, space and sequence."
~ *Libba Bray*

Occasionally we all rail against fate or life itself when we don't get what we want, when we want it, and consequently feel aggrieved and hard done by. However, when some time has passed and we look back, how many times have we realised that, when we did eventually get what we wanted, it actually arrived at the most fortuitous time for us and slotted in perfectly where and when we needed it most? Trust in Fate, Karma, whatever you personally believe in, to know best and trust that, when it's meant to happen in your life just for you, it will. Remember this, won't you?

September 9

"Sometimes good things fall apart, so better things call fall together."
~ Marilyn Monroe

Now I know this to be true because, looking back, I can see where and when it happened to me. We have all experienced times when we rail against Fate, the Universe, etc., because we feel we have been, from all the billions of people on Earth, to suffer a particular hardship, experience a troubling situation, or deal with grief. However, think about when this happened to you in the past. Now, can you recollect the days, weeks or even months that followed? Yes? Did you consequently find yourself in a better place either emotionally, physically, or financially? Well then, hopefully, instead of going "into one" the next time things do not go your way, you will wait to see how things turn out first....

September 10

"Don't count the days, make the days count." ~ *Muhammad Ali*

This reminds me of friends we had who, although they were English and resident in the UK, preferred living in the house they had bought in Florida. However, due to immigration rules they were restricted to spending 3 months in Florida then the UK for 3 months, so they made two 3 month trips every year. However, when they were in the UK, they marked the days off one by one on a calendar, and lived very frugally, preferring to save every penny for their return to Florida. This used to really "get" to me, the fact they weren't "living" life to the full because, you and I know, that nothing is certain in life especially as regards health especially when we get a bit older. They didn't care. I gave up pointing out that they would not get back the days they were so eager to cross off. They had their way of life and that was it. They have been doing it for several years now and plan to do it for several more. I will never ever understand, never!

September 11

"For success, attitude is equally as important as ability." ~ *Walter Scott*

Well of course it is! Without the right attitude to "fuel" our drive towards success we would never arrive at our chosen destination, would we? We need something to give us the "oomph" to strive for our own personal vision of success and that's where attitude comes in. Let us say you already possess all the necessary skills to achieve the success you seek. You know that is not enough, right? Without the right positive, forceful attitude to keep you going when the going gets tough (and it will trust me), you will never get anywhere, skills overload or not. So, remember to nurture the skills AND the attitude.

September 12

"Light tomorrow with today."
~ Elizabeth Barrett Browning

Lovely words, eh? I guess this just means that what we do today, if we do it well enough and with love, can be carried forward into tomorrow and, perhaps, the day after. This may not necessarily mean bringing "light" to us personally but perhaps to someone who needs it more than we do. If we all strive to generate more love, compassion, and kindness in our daily lives and in our interaction with others, then surely this will gladden our own hearts and bring us great satisfaction and a feeling of a job well done. Go on, allow your "light" to shine brightly.

September 13

"Smile….it is the key that fits the lock of everybody's heart." ~ *Anthony J. D'Angelo*

I instinctively look people in the eye when they smile at me as I have noticed that a smile does not always reach that far. I am sure many of you can relate to this too. I love it when someone smiles at me, and their smile becomes reflected in their eyes with genuine warmth, love, or friendliness. That is when you "bask" in a smile and find yourself just automatically smiling back. Your smile may just have made the day of someone who is having a bad day, feeling downhearted, lonely, or even angry! It costs you nothing but to somebody else it may be priceless.

September 14

"How people treat you is their Karma. How you react is yours." ~ *Wayne Dyer*

So true! Not everybody will respond to you in the way you expect or hope when encountering them in life. We are all different and, as such, behave and react in our own unique way. However, while we cannot control other people's behaviour towards us, we define who we are by the way in which we react to them. Just because their behaviour may not be as it should be, we should be the "bigger person" and respond in a way that is to our credit. Not always easy to do I know, but better than the alternative, don't you think?

September 15

"See the light in others and treat them as if that is all you see." ~ *Wayne Dyer*

Makes sense that, if you can see the light in others that they, in turn, will see the light in you, doesn't it? So, if we all took the time to appreciate that we ALL have light within us, some not so bright or some brighter than others because we are only human after all, wouldn't that be great? Look past the outer veneer so to speak and focus on each other's inner spark of goodness, of our shared humanity, our good points rather than our not-so-good points. Wouldn't this generate even more light for all of us? Wouldn't that be wonderful?

September 16

"It is better to walk alone, than with a crowd going in the wrong direction."
~ *Diane Grant*

Oh definitely! Only common sense if we take time to think about it. However, sometimes it is not so simple or easy for us to break away from the wrong-footed crowd once we are part of it and being swept along by it. Brilliant for those of us aware enough to realise that's what is happening and are taking steps to break free to walk our own path even if it is alone so a wee bit scary, even for the more confident among us. At least, as we stand alone and watch the misguided crowd continue without us into the distance, we know we are now free to choose the direction in life WE want to aim for so, what are YOU waiting for?

September 17

"Real success is finding your life work in the work that you love."
~ David McCullough

I can soooo relate to this! I have been blessed that, following early retirement, I have found my niche in working with Tarot. I do not consider it "work," as I feel blessed to be able to do what I love most every day. However, I do realise that not all of us are so fortunate. Many people wake up each morning dreading the day ahead in a job they really dislike but feel trapped with no choice because of a need to earn money to pay their way through life. Let's face it, most of us need to earn a living. Real success is being able to do something you love, which also generates enough money to pay the bills. So, if you can or have achieved this for yourself, be sure to give thanks every day that you are one of the incredibly lucky ones.

September 18

"What day is it, asked Pooh? It's today, squeaked Piglet. My favourite day, said Pooh." ~ *A.A. Milne*

Out of the mouths of babes and bears! With the right attitude, every day has the propensity to be a favourite day. Just the fact that you are fortunate enough to have woken up following bedtime the night before is a big plus, isn't it? Of course, it is! So, make sure you fully appreciate the rest of your day as the special gift it is, and thoroughly enjoy everything and everybody in it, as who knows what tomorrow will bring.......

September 19

"Curiosity will conquer fear even more than bravery will." ~ *James Stephens*

Curiosity plays a large part in human nature and always has, ever since the beginning of time. No curiosity would have meant no inventions, no exploration of our planet or others, no medicine, or advances in anything and everything. Things we take for granted today in our daily lives would not exist because nobody was curious enough to take the first step to invent or discover them. I could go on, but you get the gist, don't you? Our curiosity is what drives us to persevere in discovering and exploring while conquering and overruling our own fears in the process. Whew! We owe a great deal to our curiosity, don't we? Thank goodness for curiosity I say!

September 20

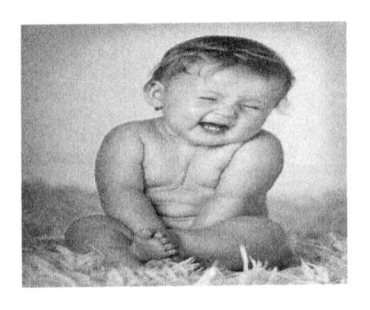

"A laugh is a smile that bursts."
~ Mary H. Waldrip

I love this, don't you? It made me smile when I came across it as I can see how this would make sense. It really made me think too. A laugh does grow from a smile, doesn't it? Not always, I know, but it must start somewhere and where better than a smile? I always think that a smile given freely can mean more to the person on the receiving end than the "smiler" will ever know. That is why I tend to smile at everybody I interact with during my day because knowing how much a smile can mean to me makes me realise that it may be the same for someone else. Even better if it bursts into a laugh...

September 21

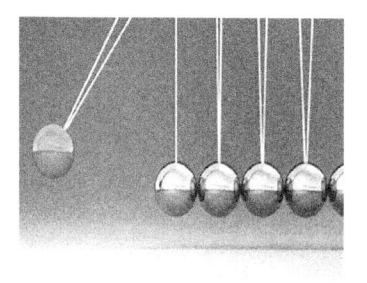

"Everything we do affects other people."
~ Luke Ford

Of course, it does! Think about it logically.... Every single thing we do has a reaction or a consequence, not only for us, but for other people. The type of action taken also defines the repercussions, i.e., minor, or major, which will also impact those closest to us or people we have never, and will never, meet. Like a stone thrown into a still pond, the ripples will continue to reach outwards affecting everything they touch, just like our actions will. Something for us all to think about in the future.

September 22

"We don't meet people by accident. They are meant to cross our path for a reason."
~ *Kathryn Perez*

I have always believed this to be true. There have been so many people in my life who have made an impact, taught me a lesson, perhaps welcome perhaps not, but necessary, or enhanced my journey through life, etc., that it cannot, just cannot, be just "chance." I am very aware that I may not realise it at the time of our coming together, but I always do at some point in the future. Like most people, I did not think about this much, if at all, to be honest. However, too many things have caused me to look at when, where and how certain people came to be part of my life and realise how "meant" their presence was and is. Look around you. See what I mean?

September 23

"A hug is a great gift – one size fits all, and it's easy to exchange." ~ *Unknown*

This makes me smile as everybody who knows me is aware that I am a serial hugger and, bless them, few flee in panic now when they see me coming towards them, arms outstretched. Indeed, many people, although not expecting it, seem ready to welcome a hug and reciprocate in kind. It is like a universal language in saying "I like/love you because you are a hug-worthy person." It is a mutual expression of just showing you care enough about someone to share a hug. So go on, off you go and look for somebody to hug, you know you want to!

September 24

"Nothing ever goes away until it teaches us what we need to know." ~ *Pema Chodron*

We have all gone through challenging times in life, haven't we? Times when we feel that Fate, Karma, whatever, has singled us out to "get us!" That feeling of "it's just not fair!" I have had my fair share, believe me! However, looking back, I realise that I reached the other side of whatever it was, having learned a valuable lesson for the future. Being so caught up in the situation, at the time, I could not see the "bigger picture." Now, when faced with a "situation" I know there will be a lesson in there somewhere and, although it may not be obvious to me at the time, I will become aware when the time is right. An "Oh I get it" moment!

❁

September 25

"When you judge another, you do not define them, you define yourself."
~ Wayne Dyer

This asks us to look at ourselves when we are inclined or tempted to judge other people. Sometimes we can be very judgemental, can't we? I know I can. However, I really understand what this is saying. Every one of us is defined by the words or actions we use to judge someone else, usually without really getting to know them, or being able to get to know them. How many times have you judged someone, then got to know them better, and reversed your initial judgement? What do you think of the person you were when you made that judgement? Exactly! Get it now?

September 26

"Never limit your views of life by any past experience." ~ *Ernest Holmes*

Not an easy thing to do by any means, is it? Past experiences, whether good or bad, can colour the way we perceive things in the future, that's just human nature. However, by allowing this to happen we unwittingly put restrictions in place and that is not good, is it? We deserve better, so be kind to yourself, and leave what is already in the past where it belongs, in the past. There is no way you would be silly enough to allow it power over your future now is there? Of course not!

September 27

"In the practice of tolerance, one's enemy is the best teacher." ~ *Dalai Lama*

Made me smile because, although it took me a minute to make sense of, it then made perfect sense. Let's face it, who would test your tolerance more than your enemy? Nobody, that's who! Just by learning to deflect or deal with whatever comes at you from someone who does not regard you as "flavour of the month," in a calm and mature way, will test your tolerance limits big time. So, you should be thanking whoever it is in a way, shouldn't you, for teaching you to be the tolerant person you are today. Well, maybe not!

September 28

"Be not afraid of growing slowly, be afraid only of standing still." ~ *Chinese Proverb*

No one on our beautiful planet knows everything about everything. Saying that, every new day does present every one of us with opportunities and the potential to learn and to grow as human beings. However, occasionally, we may tend to be impatient because we feel we are not learning as fast as we think we could or should, perhaps comparing ourselves unfavourably with other people. However, look on the positive side, at least we are taking steps to actively learn and progress. We are not choosing to be at a standstill! Every second, every minute, every hour, every day, brings us closer to what we dream of achieving just for us. So, take heart and carry on...

September 29

**"The truth you believe and cling to makes
you unavailable to hear anything new."**
~ Pema Chodrun

*This reminds me of kids who do not want to hear
what they are being told so stick their fingers in
their ears and sing loudly! I guess we can all be
like these kids at times. We all have our own
opinions on anything and everything and, once we
have formed our opinion on certain topics or
certain people then that is it! A done deal! So,
well done us, eh? We have effectively prevented
ourselves from ever having to rethink or change
what we have set in stone. So, what does that
make us? Definitely not the brightest bulbs in the
box!*

September 30

"The cave you fear to enter holds the treasure you seek." ~ *Joseph Campbell*

All of us have been afraid at times so fear is not a stranger. It may have prevented us from doing something that was not in our best interest but, on the other hand, it may also have stopped us from experiencing something wonderful. The trick is to know which is which. We have all felt the fear that makes our heart beat a little faster and presses our "fight or flight" button, usually before doing something that makes us nervous, or meeting someone that we are unsure of. However, trust that the fear is saying it's okay to be a bit afraid as it will keep you alert and, on your toes, but NEVER let it stop you from doing something that may be the greatest experience of your life, or meeting someone who could prove to be the key to your future happiness.

October

300

October 1

"Sometimes our greatest insight comes from our failure, not from our accomplishments." ~ *Mark Cuban*

When we accomplish or achieve our goals too easily, or we never fail in our attempts at success, often we stop thinking too much about putting so much hard work in or we become complacent about our accomplishments. However, when we do fail, only then do we begin to wonder why we failed and what we need to do differently in order to achieve success again in the future. Failure allows us the opportunity to stop, examine, and rethink. This can lead us to greater insight than before and enable us to realize how precious our accomplishments really are.

October 2

"Do your little bit of good where you are; it's those little bits of good put together that overwhelm the world."
~ *Desmond Tutu*

Perhaps we feel insignificant in the world? That nothing we say or do matters very much in the grand scheme of things? However, let's imagine that everybody on the planet actually took time to say hello and smile at a stranger, or lend a hand to somebody needing help. Perhaps just listening with compassion, or without being judgmental, to someone's tale of woe. Wow! How amazing would that be? How many people would be touched and comforted by an act of kindness by someone close to them or by a stranger? Think what a happy planet this would and could be for us all. If only…...

October 3

"The longer you wait for the future, the shorter it will be." ~ *Loesje*

Of course, it will! Stands to reason, doesn't it? The longer you wait for the future, the longer your past will be so you do not have to be Einstein to figure out that the future will be shorter! A heads up to stop procrastinating, dithering or being indecisive. Decide who you want to be and what you want to achieve in your future and then do your best to take the steps necessary to achieve it. A definite bonus would be to begin the process while you still have more of the future than the past.

October 4

"When life knocks you down, roll over and look at the stars." ~ *Unknown*

I love this quote. I always think that perhaps life is knocking you down for just that reason.... you need to lie there, lose yourself in the wonderful cosmos above, enjoy and wonder at the twinkling stars and astral bodies and just be...... Of course, I guess it also means that when life gets troublesome, difficult, or just plain nasty, it is more comforting isn't it to believe that it's going to get better, it will pass, and we'll be happy again. Remember that old song, "When you wish upon a star.......?" Lovely!

October 5

"Letting go gives us freedom, and freedom is the only condition for happiness. If, in our heart, we still cling to anything – anger, anxiety or possessions – we cannot be free." ~ *Thich Nhat Hanh*

Holding on to anger, anxiety, possessions or indeed issues from the past or the present, tethers us with an invisible cord of our own making. This prevents us from being free to live our lives the way they should be lived, full of joy, fulfilment and happiness. Fortunately, the power to cut this cord and gain our freedom lies within each of us so we need to take control by grasping the scissors firmly and severing the cord forever. We can then breathe a sigh of relief while watching it disappear back to wherever it came from forever, and consequently feel totally free to embrace and enjoy our newfound freedom with happy hearts and minds.

October 6

"Minds are like parachutes, they only function when open." ~ *Frank Zappa*

Over time, our minds naturally fill with opinions, the minutia of day to day living, etc., until we have set ideas and opinions on most things and the people and situations, we experience daily. We tend not to be as open as we were when we were younger as we've spent years storing things in our minds that we believe will serve us well in life. Basically, we're closed to what life has to offer. However, once we realize that an open mind offers us very many more possibilities, so many more opportunities to embrace new experiences, exciting ideas, and to learn and continue learning. Never forget, an open mind is a healthy mind.

October 7

"Look for something <u>positive</u> in each day, even if some days you have to look a little harder." ~ *Unknown*

There are days you wish you had just stayed in bed aren't there? The day may get off to a bad start. Perhaps stepping out of bed into a pool of cat/dog wee, stubbing your toe on the bathroom door, dropping your cereal bowl, etc. Then it goes from bad to worse as the day progresses. Everything you touch either burns or breaks. Nothing mechanical works the way it should and, to make it worse, you feel as if you are coming down with something and do not feel 100%. Then somebody annoyingly cheerful comes along and advises you to look on the bright side of things. When you have successfully restrained yourself from making them a lot less cheerful, perhaps you should take their advice and take time to look on the bright side. I am sure there will be something in your day that will cause you to smile and feel happy even just for a short time, so why not be grateful for whatever it is and, who knows, your day could start to improve.

October 8

"Broken crayons still colour."
~ David Weaver

It is so easy to say, "I'd do this if I had (fill in the blanks)" or "I can't do this because I don't have (fill in the blanks)." The truth is, we all possess the tools we need every day to do the things we dream of. If we are feeling broken by life, we still retain the power to power to "colour" and create the life we want. Of course, we do and, by being determined and focused on continuing to fill our lives with the colours we choose, e.g., people, pursuits, goals, whatever "crayon" we use, we manifest the "colouring book" of the life we picture exists and lies ahead for us. The brighter and more vivid the better. Sounds like a plan, doesn't it?

October 9

"I can't change the direction of the wind, but I can adjust my sails to always reach my destination." ~ *Jimmy Dean*

We have no control over the winds of life and, indeed, are at their mercy as to where they send us. However, being aware that this is life as we know it and taking steps to adjust our outlook and our plans as and when necessary, means that being off-course now and then need not lead to disaster. Being prepared to adjust and change when we need to would allow us to continue regardless of where we find ourselves and, indeed, if not enjoy the experience, to at least cope with it while it lasts.

October 10

"Man cannot discover new oceans unless he has the courage to lose sight of the shore." ~ *Andre Gide*

It's not easy to cast ourselves adrift and trust that things will be okay, and we won't come to any harm on the way to where we will ultimately end up. However, let's just think about this for a moment. Do we really want to be stuck where we are forever? Never making new discoveries about us or others. Never feeling the flutter in our tummies that we get when we know something exciting is about to happen or when we take a chance or a risk in life? Sometimes it's good to just "let go" and "cast off" to discover the other shores out there that we've yet to explore. Who knows what awaits us?

October 11

"A real friend is one who walks in when the rest of the world walks out."
~ *Walter Winchell*

I guess we've all been in a situation where we find out who our true friends are. You know the scenario, we're in financial trouble, our relationship isn't working, or our work situation is becoming precarious. So, what do we do? We call our friends and ask for their help. Sometimes it's just for reassurance that things will get better and to hear, "hey, I'm always here for you." Other times we ask for financial aid just for a short while until things improve It's at times like these that people, we believed to be friends may fade into the background, maybe because they don't want to be put on the spot, they're dealing with their own issues, or just because they don't think enough about you to really care. This is when your true friends count. The ones who may also have problems but who care enough about you to help you out and make sure you know you can count on them. True friends indeed, treasure them.

October 12

"Today is the tomorrow you worried about yesterday." ~ *Dale Carnegie*

My lovely Dad used to have a saying, "You worry, you die," You don't worry, you die, so why worry?" If only it were that simple? None of us want to worry do we? We don't want to be tossing and turning at night and struggling to get through the day because of worry but, we're human beings, and it's something we do whether we choose to or not. However, if we can distance ourselves just a little and think "outside the box" we would realise that worrying doesn't help resolve anything at all. There's no easy answer as to how to stop yourself worrying but remember everything passes.... Nothing stays the same whether we waste time worrying or not.

❧

October 13

"Conformity is the jailer of freedom and the enemy of hope." ~ *John F. Kennedy*

Some of us spend our whole lives fitting in with everybody else's rules, regulations, beliefs, etc., and perhaps don't even realise we're doing it as it's the way we've always done things and what's wrong with that? However, sometimes it's good to shake off conformity and actually do what you want for a change. So, what if you feel like taking a day off work during the week to walk in the woods or just going on a shopping spree? Instead of spending your weekends doing the same old, same old, do something different, something more adventurous. This might be the beginning of a new phase in your life that brings you joy and freedom to be yourself, so what are you waiting for...?"

October 14

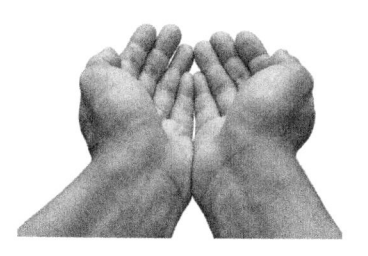

"Feeling gratitude and not expressing it is like wrapping a present and not giving it."
~ *William Arthur Ward*

Life, for most of us, is lived in a rush. Deadlines, having to be somewhere at a certain time, having dinner on the table in the evening, picking up the kids, and Doctor/Dentist appointments...It's so easy to forget to be grateful, not just to people who have done something for us, but to the world, the universe, nature, and what you believe in that gives you strength and hope. Take the time to give thanks for all you have, your family, the good health you enjoy, the world you live and in, that you have a comfortable home and food on the table. Giving thanks brings so much to us when we remember to express it. Unwrap this very special present and give.

October 15

"A new outlook brightens your image and brings new friends." ~ *Unknown*

There's nothing better than discovering a new hobby or joining a group of like-minded people in exploring the world of literature, the countryside, places of historical interest, or taking an interest in what's around you. We can become settled in our ways and forget that there is a wonderful world out there filled with exciting possibilities just waiting for us to stir ourselves and actually do something about it. When we do.... well, why didn't we do this before? What were we waiting for? Our new friends will bring new life to us and be happy to accompany us on our adventures to come. How wonderful is that?

October 16

**"It is our choices that show what we truly
are, far more than our abilities."
~ *J.K. Rowling***

We are all born with our own individual, unique abilities and, as we travel through life, we alone choose how to build on these and use them on our journey. However, it's the choices we make in how we use our abilities that define us. We can either choose to use them with honourable intentions or, alternatively, not so honourable intentions. It is this individual intent that the outside world becomes aware of and therefore knows exactly what we are all about, i.e., where we are coming from and where we are going, and judges us accordingly. Something to remember.

October 17

**"Fear does not have any special power
unless you empower it by submitting to it."
~ *Les Brown***

Being afraid is not always a bad thing as it's our own in-built warning system about real or perceived danger, so we should always acknowledge the reason we feel afraid. However, on the other hand, sometimes it is too easy to allow fear to overwhelm us and perhaps prevent us from doing something we want to that yes, may cause us to be fearful but which, in the long run, could enhance our lives. When we allow fear to dictate what we do or don't do, we restrict the failures and triumphs we may experience so, to quote an old saying, "Feel the fear and do it anyway."

October 18

"It's not what happens to you, it's what you do about it." ~ *W. Mitchell*

I've always believed that things that happen to us happen for a reason. Whether we choose to make the most of it or think "poor me" is up to the individual. All of us have at one time or another, experienced relationship problems, suffered a personal loss, financial hardship, family or work issues, etc. We are all different in how we deal with what life throws at us. If we can retain a "glass half full" rather than a "glass half empty" ethic, then we're on our way to, not, only dealing with our problems and moving on, but building on our ability to do so again in the future hopefully in the process, also making it easier to do than the previous occasion.

October 19

"We are not human beings on a spiritual journey, we are spiritual beings on a human journey." ~ *Stephen Covey*

Oh, I so agree with this! I believe we are all spiritual beings and that our journey through life as a human is something we are asked to do and tasked with by a Higher Power. The trials and tribulations each of us experience is pre-ordained, although how we each deal with these is not. This is our path to navigate to the best of our ability using the tools we are gifted with at birth, and every step we take, every lesson we learn, is recognised, and recorded. Our purpose is to learn as it's all about how much we learn, how we learn, what we do with what we learn.... no more no less.

October 20

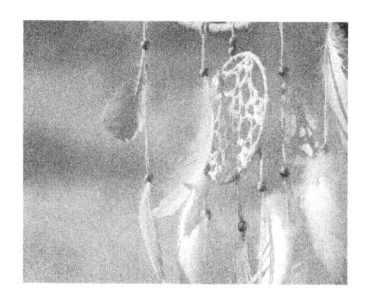

**"Always remember to fall asleep with a
dream and wake up with a purpose."
~ *Gabby Bernstein***

*If you're anything like me when I fall asleep the
thoughts going round in my head are to do with
the many tasks I have to do the following day or,
occasionally, my favourite movie star begging me
for a date (not!) However, wouldn't it be
wonderful to fall asleep with plans for a new
adventure, an exciting new venture involving a
dream you've had for a while or a holiday
somewhere you've always wanted to go but never
got round to. Well, what's stopping you? Make
tonight the night you fall asleep with the intention
of making your dreams a reality and wake up
tomorrow raring to begin! Up to you!*

October 21

"Everything you've ever wanted is on the other side of fear." ~ *George Addair*

Isn't it a pity when we have so many dreams we want to realize and the only thing stopping us is our fear of failure? We listen to other people, perhaps more opinionated or more confident than us, giving us perhaps unasked for advice that they think we need to conquer our fear and just go for what we want. Not that easy for some of us though, is it? Think about it though. We either determine what we want and plan how to go about getting it, or we fail before we start by being afraid. Do we really want the "f" word to win? Of course, we don't, we want the "s" (success) word to win so push fear aside and reach for success, and you may be surprised!

October 22

"Don't judge each day by the harvest you reap, but by the seeds you plant."
~ Robert Louis Stevenson

At the end of our day when we recall how the time passed and how we filled the hours, do we think more of what we got from the day or what we put into it? Perhaps your "harvest" is represented by the money you earned for a job well done, praise for a meal you cooked or accomplishing a goal etc. These are all transitory events while, making a new friend, beginning a course of learning, or gaining a new skill will plant a seed we can grow and nurture forever. What will you do tomorrow?

October 23

"Be somebody who makes everybody feel like a somebody." ~ *Brad Montague*

We have all run across those people who make us feel special, and they can be rare indeed. So often we are all focused on our own little world, our current problems, or our goals that we miss the opportunity to stop and just "be." If you look around for someone who could use an encouraging word, some attention or even just a smile, it will not take you long to find them. And I can assure you that, if you take one minute a day to uplift someone else, you will feel wonderful the rest of the day!

October 24

"If you love life, life will love you back."
~ Arthur Rubinstein

Isn't that nice to know? I think it's very easy for us all to get so caught up in just living day-to-day and dealing with all our commitments, jobs, and responsibilities that we tend to forget how fortunate we are just to be alive. We need to make a conscious effort to rediscover the joy of life. The pleasure we get from the company and love of our family and friends, a good book, and doing something we enjoy that gives us pleasure. When we are able, and indeed willing, to do this, we open up and allow life to bring the joy and excitement that we have perhaps, through neglect, let slip away and return to fill our waking hours with the happiness and sense of wellbeing we have been lacking. This is a good thing...right?

October 25

**"I am not what has happened to me. I am
what I choose to become."**
~ Carl Gustav Jung

*Anybody who remarks that life has not shaped
them is fooling themselves. Life shapes us from
the moment we first draw breath. The remarkable
thing is that we are able, through our own
actions, to absorb how and what we learn, how
we relate to other people or situations, how we
progress through our life path. We learn lessons
along the way, some easily learned, some not so
easily. Every action, every experience shapes us
into who we choose to become. I say choose
because we are, to a certain extent, masters of our
own destinies, so it's down to us what we retain
and what we discard in order to grow into the best
we can be in life. Our choice, our life.*

October 26

"Don't let someone who has done nothing tell you how to do anything." ~ *Steve Martin*

I know a lot of people who are quick to offer me advice even if I haven't asked for it. They are adamant that they are the only person in the whole world who knows exactly how I can solve my problem, my issue or reach the right decision. However, the truth is that they don't, in fact, have anything realistic or helpful to offer me because they have never experienced my situation personally. They may be acting with what they believe are good intentions and that's fair enough. However, when I want advice, I want it from people I trust and that I know have been through similar, if not the same, issues and who have learned a lesson from it, so I know they have the experience to help me help myself. That's sensible, isn't it?

October 27

**"There is a difference between giving up
and knowing when you have had enough."**
~ Sushan Sharma

*We've all been there, haven't we? Something or
someone in our life causing us to struggle in an
effort to stay strong and battle through in moving
forward. Sometimes it's not too much of a struggle
but, at other times, we can find ourselves facing a
major, unrelenting energy and soul sapping
problem. When that happens, we often get to a
point where continuing would be futile and cause
more harm and/or grief than it's worth. It's being
able to realize this and act on it that enables us to
just walk away or distance ourselves. This is
acting through strength not weakness.*

October 28

**"Don't get upset with people or situations;
both are powerless without your reaction."**
~ *Unknown*

*Absolutely true don't you think? However, it is not
easy for most of us not to react when people or a
situation causes us to be upset. I can see the logic
here though. If we do allow whatever is
happening to provoke a response then we are
giving them/it what it was hoping for when they/it
said or did to us, ergo they/it win! Sounds
convoluted I know but take time to think about it
and you will see what I mean. So, next time you
feel yourself getting upset, take a deep breath,
count to 10, 20 or, if it is a real humdinger, to 100,
and hopefully the response you give, or do not
give, will be one in the eye for your own personal
upset, so there!*

October 29

"Not everyone you lose is a loss."
~ Paulo Coelho

Well, I guess we can all relate to this although not all of us will have realised it at the time. Have you ever bemoaned the fact that someone you considered family, friend, a lover, a trusted colleague, has stepped away from you and left you wondering what just happened? Perhaps there was no explanation for their departure or, if there was, maybe you disagreed with their reasons and begged them to stay around. However, when you have looked back, sometime in the future, how many times have you realised that they did you a favour and you should get down on your knees and thank your lucky stars that you "lost" them when you did. Whew!

October 30

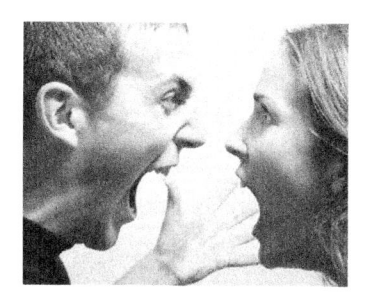

"Anger is a feeling that makes your mouth work faster." ~ *Unknown*

Much, much faster and our poor brain is probably in panic mode, desperately trying to get the message, "Please don't speak until I sort this out" through to us. Do we listen? Probably not. Anger is the fuel which stokes the flames of our vocabulary spectacularly! So easy just to let rip, isn't it? Satisfying too! However, once we've said our piece and calmed down just tad, perhaps whoever has borne the brunt of our "flames" looks so dejected and hurt that, being the lovely person we really are, we begin to wish that we could take, if not all, at least some of what we've said in anger back? In fact, we may have reacted without knowing the full facts or the whole story. So, perhaps the next time our ire rises we should take time to, 1. Engage brain, 2. Think, 3. Mouth, 4. Speak.... or not?

October 31

"Make today count, you'll never get it back." ~ *Unknown*

Now this is good advice and worth following, don't you think? However, I guess, like me and most people, we do not often take the time to think along these lines. We are too busy going about our daily lives and dealing with whatever the days bring us. Some days are wonderful and some days we just want to be over. Keep in mind though, when you wake in the morning, which is a gift in itself, that the day ahead only lasts for a mere 24 hours and then it has gone FOREVER! So, whatever it brings, it is unique, a never to be repeated special offer, so make sure you take full advantage.

November

November 1

"When looking back doesn't interest you anymore, you're doing something right."
~ Unknown

Well done if you feel this quote says it all for you! None of us travel through life without accumulating "baggage" along the way. This can either be baggage you are happy to shoulder and carry with you or, on the other hand, baggage that you would rather discard to the dim and distant Lost Property Office of Life's Railway Station and throw away the ticket. If it is the latter, then you are truly extremely fortunate and will find yourself being able to anticipate the future and what it holds for you without relics of an unfortunate, troubling past, nipping at your ankles like a small bad-tempered canine. Well done!

November 2

"To wish you were someone else is to waste the person you are." ~ *Kurt Cobain*

Of course, it is and why would you be so misguided? Of course, you wouldn't! Here you are, a unique, individual human being with your own personality, gifts, and talents, which everybody who knows and loves you appreciates totally, because it is YOU! So, instead of trying to emulate somebody else, who is not fit to lick your boots by the way, pay homage to your Creator by being the wonderful person you were made to be.

November 3

"Life is all about finding people who are your kind of crazy." ~ *Unknown*

Oh, I've fortunately found mine. What about you? I hope you have people in your life who add that little zing to whatever you do, who encourage you to stand out from the crowd and who "get" who you are totally and without judgement. People you have felt an instant connection with perhaps because of a shared sense of humour, or something you are both enthusiastic about. Whatever the reason, there is a mutual need to connect. Isn't it wonderful to just be yourself and know that your like-minded friends cherish and value your presence in their lives just as you value theirs? I know I am very blessed, and I expect you do too...don't you?

November 4

"Life doesn't get better by chance; it gets better by change." ~ *Jim Rohn*

My mantra has always been, "If you don't ask, you don't get" so this resonates with me on a personal level. Makes sense doesn't it that, if you decide what you want in life and take positive steps to make it a reality, then who is to say you will not succeed. At least you have tried so, if you do not get want you want, (this time), you can console yourself with the knowledge that you did what you could, and it just was not meant to be (this time). Much, much better to act when and where YOU decide to rather than allowing yourself to be putty in the hands of Fate. Now, what would you rather do? Thought so! Well done!

November 5

"A head full of fears has no space for dreams." ~ *Deborah Evans*

That would be our imagination working against us rather than for us. Filling our heads with the fear of things that may never happen, situations or feelings which might entrap us, fear of failure, ridicule, etc., etc., etc. Hold on a minute.... If our heads are full of only negativity and fear where is the space holding our dreams? Nowhere that's where? Doesn't that sound awful? So, what should we do? Allow fear to hog all the space? No, I do not think so either! So, let us all just spend some time decluttering, or should I say defearing? Good riddance fear and hello dreams, we hope you will be comfortable in your new home and decide to stay forever.

November 6

"When a friend does something wrong, don't forget all the things they did right."
~ Unknown

Of course, you won't! Lovely person that you are. When a friend does something, we consider wrong, that is when we remember all the things, they have done for us in the past. The times they have given us a shoulder to cry on, hugged us when we have needed a hug, been patient when it is obvious, we are driving them loopy, loaned us money when we're hard up. The list goes on and on, doesn't it? Also, this is the perfect time to think about the boot being on the other foot so to speak! If, positions were reversed, wouldn't we expect our friends to take the time to think about all the good things we have done for them…. Of course, we would, so there is your answer… simple!

November 7

"Blessed are those who can give without remembering and take without forgetting."
~ Elizabeth Bibesco

I think this is the type of person we all aspire to and believe ourselves to be. You know what I mean. We can give freely with no strings attached, no hidden agenda, and then forget about it, happy just to have been in a position to help out. However, when we ourselves need some help, either emotionally or financially, we never forget who gave freely to us and ensure we always carry this with us and are happy to repay our debt should the opportunity present itself.

November 8

"Nobody can hurt me without my permission." ~ *Mahatma Gandhi*

Says it all doesn't it? Nobody <u>can</u> hurt you without your permission. This does not mean telling someone who wants to hurt you, "Yes, you have my permission to hurt me." "Go right ahead." "Do your worst." What it does mean is that nobody can hurt you, either mentally or physically, if you refuse to give them that power over you, i.e., allowing yourself to feel "hurt." Of course, they can cause you pain physically, but only you can choose to feel "hurt." The power is yours and yours alone so use it wisely.

❁

November 9

"Anxiety does not empty tomorrow of its sorrows, but only empties today of its strength." ~ *Charles Spurgeon*

This is a no brainer, right? We are all aware that spending our days being anxious and weighed down with worry and stress accomplishes absolutely nothing. We have all been there, haven't we? Easy for others to say "don't worry" but we can't help it. It is as if our minds have been taken over by that evil supervillain, "Anxiety!" At times like that we have to call on our own superhero, "So what?" This is because we know that giving in to "Anxiety" gives it the power to suck the joy and light from our day and replace it with darkness. This achieves absolutely nothing in the way of solving whatever is worrying us in our todays and tomorrows so, next time that nasty "Anxiety" looms, call on your own personal superhero, "So what" and see it off pronto! Ta dah!

November 10

"I'd rather regret the things I've done than regret the things I haven't done."
~ Lucille Ball

Wouldn't we all? It must be awful to be about to pass to Spirit and your mind is filled, not with happy recollections of all the things you have done in your life but regret for the things you did not. Too late then my friends. Let us hope that you are among the lucky ones who realised early on in life that they wanted to follow their dreams, explore this beautiful Earth, love with all their heart, take leaps of faith, etc. Better to be among the real winners at the end of the ultimate game than the losers. I know which one I will be. Do you?

November 11

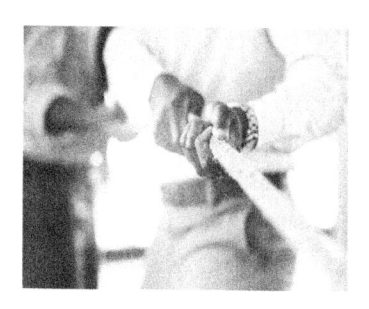

"Givers need to set limits because Takers rarely do." ~ *Rachel Wolchin*

We all know the "takers" in our lives, don't we? The people who always want somebody else to do what they may be too lazy to do themselves. Always short of money although not when it comes to the luxuries in life. Expecting others to drop whatever they are doing and rush to their aid. I could go on, but I think you have all got the picture and already have images of people like this known to you popping into your head. I know I have. I speak from experience when I say it is not easy to break the pattern of always saying, "Yes, of course" but, trust me, it can be done. Ask yourself if they would do the same for you? No? Then it is up to you to establish boundaries. The next time the "taker" asks you for something, take a deep breath, and say "no" and mean it. They won't like it but at least it will let them know that the "worm has turned" and is not always ready, willing, and able. After the first refusal, you will find it gets easier to say no and, hopefully, they

345

*will get the hint and find another mug 'er "Giver"
and leave you alone = result!*

❁

November 12

"Learn to say "no" without explaining yourself." ~ *Paulo Coelho*

I think we all find it natural when we say no to follow it with a reason, i.e. "I've a dental appointment, visiting a friend, short of funds, a previous engagement, etc. Just force of habit really, believing that we need to explain as our refusal needs justifying by softening the blow for whoever is asking. However, this can become tricky as there cannot be many of us who have not been caught out in a white lie at some time or another. Even if you have a legitimate reason for refusing, there is no rule that says you must explain yourself or else! So, if you want to say no, just say it. No excuses. There, feel better? Good.

November 13

"By being yourself, you put something wonderful in the world that wasn't there before." ~ *Unknown*

How much time do we spend comparing ourselves to others? I wish I had her hair, his money, their house... When we do this, our serenity and inner peace go right out the window! Instead of lamenting what you don't have, turn your perspective around by acknowledging the unique and wonderful presence you bring to the world. Whatever we focus on grows stronger, so make it a point today just to be yourself and continue to share your "specialty" with those you encounter today.

❁

November 14

"Your attitude, not your aptitude, will determine your altitude." ~ *Zig Ziglar*

This has a ring to it doesn't it? So true too and quite simple to understand. It is your attitude that determines how you will get through life and how high you will fly, not the skills you possess. You may have mastered your craft and be very talented or gifted but, if you view and live your life with the wrong attitude, it is very unlikely you will ever experience "lift off" and the stars will always remain out of reach which is such a shame don't you think when, just by changing the way you look at things, could help you reach your own personal star.

November 15

"Positive anything is better than negative nothing." ~ *Elbert Hubbard*

Of course, it is! In fact, being positive is what gets most of us out of bed in the morning and keeps us motivated throughout our day. The trick is to hold onto it and keep holding on no matter what negativity we experience, either from people or situations. You have a choice. Determine to be positive in thought and action and therefore have peace of mind knowing you have done your best or, think negatively about who or what you are experiencing and sink further into the pit of total negativity and helplessness? Surely, it serves us better to follow the former option? Onwards and upwards my friends! Who is with me?

November 16

"I'm going to make the rest of my life, the best of my life." ~ *Unknown*

This should be a mantra for everybody to follow. It does not matter what has gone before in your life, how old you are, what you possess or do not possess, who you know…. Just to have the insight to realise that, with your own thoughts and actions, YOU have the power to ensure that every day, from this day forward, can be the first of many best days of the rest of your life. How amazingly liberating is that? It may take us a long time to learn that every day we live is a gift but the fact that we have gained this insight leaves us no excuse for then not living life to the full from the very second, we do…no excuse whatsoever.

November 17

"Stop letting people who do so little for you control so much of your mind, feelings and emotions." ~ *Will Smith*

I guess we have all been guilty of this at some time or another, I know I have. Sometimes we are just too nice, too trusting, and too easily led. Over time, it may become a pattern and a way of life so that we just fall into going along with somebody else's perception of how we should feel or react. Perhaps it is time for a personal "wake up call" when we all take a moment to stop and think if this relates to someone in our lives? If so, time to take charge. Initially, it may not be easy to put this into practice but persevere, as once you have learned this lesson, you will not need any revision in the future.

November 18

"The happiest people do not have the best of everything. They make the best of everything they have." ~ *Roy T. Bennett*

What a wonderful way to live your life isn't it? Believing the best in other people, appreciating what you do have rather than bemoaning what you don't? Our society seems totally fixated and focused on the latest designer handbag/shoes, clothes, watch, and jewellery; we should be wearing. The "in" places we should be partying or eating at, blah, blah, blah! Pictures of "celebrities," and I use the term very loosely here, whom we are led to believe are living lives we should all aspire to! Not me, thank you very much. I fully appreciate what I have and am very happy and content with what life continues to gift me. I'll wager you are just the same?

❁

November 19

"Every day do something that will inch you closer to a better tomorrow."
~ Roy T. Bennett

Now this needn't be a daily grand gesture but more along the lines of progressive self-help. Be mindful each day to try and accomplish a small goal. For example, you could take steps to overcome a bad habit, embark on a course of learning, learn a new skill, etc. Perhaps also doing something for others, e.g., a kind gesture, an unselfish act, or being generous with either your time or money. You get the idea? By determining and achieving goals you have set and performing small acts of kindness towards others, perhaps less fortunate than you, you are steadily and continually building your character, who you are, and who you will be. This can, not only improve all of your tomorrows, but all the tomorrows of others too.

November 20

"Let your past make you better not bitter."
~ Unknown

Painful lessons learned the hard way from the past can very easily colour our present with bitterness. We have all, at one time or another, experienced troubling situations, relationship problems, failure, despair, loss, etc. However, it is how we each deal with our own personal "demons from the past" that defines our future. There is <u>always</u> a lesson to be learned from a painful past and, however bitter it is, accept what it has to teach you and be grateful for the insight gained for the future. Full marks if you do!

November 21

**"Live in such a way that if someone spoke
badly of you, no one would believe it."
~ *Zig Ziglar***

*I may be totally deluded or having a "senior
moment," but I believe most people do try to live
their lives by being the type of person that other
people speak kindly of. I know I try to, and I
imagine you do too. Living your life, mindful of
the feelings of others, showing kindness and
compassion, being honourable in whatever you
do, being loyal, all paints a picture of how the
people you know "see" you. So, if your portrait
does you justice and it is one that people respect
and admire, then woe betide anyone who speaks
badly or disparagingly of you. Isn't that a nice
thought?*

November 22

"Positive mind, Positive vibes, Positive life." ~ *Unknown*

Sounds like a simple sum doesn't it, Positive mind + Positive vibes = Positive life! I suppose, thinking about it a bit more, the result is a no brainer! However, it is not so easy for many of us to feel positive, especially if we feel that Life has been strewing one obstacle after another in our path. We have all been there at one time or another and just when we think we have successfully overcome a problem and are halfway to breathing a sigh of relief, even before we can exhale, something else pops up to take its place! Well, all we can do is grit our teeth, pop a positive thought in our mind, allow it to generate positive vibes and of we go again! Positive life here we come!

November 23

"Be a fruit loop in a world full of cherries."
~ Unknown

Isn't it wonderful being just a tad different from everybody else in the herd? Something that makes you stand out and be noticed! Your own individual quirk or unique personality trait. I know so many "cherries" who are happy and content just to be cherries and I am very happy for them. However, that is not for me, no sirree! I don't think I could be a cherry even if I wanted to. What about you, are you a cherry or a fruit loop? If you feel you are the former, why not give yourself permission to be the latter? You never know, you might enjoy yourself and discover a new lease of life. The bowl is more than large enough for all of us, and we promise to budge up for you so what are you waiting for? Fruit loops rule!!

November 24

"Your hardest times often lead to the greatest moments of your life. Keep going. Tough situations build strong people in the end." ~ *Roy. T. Bennett*

They certainly do! This reminds me of another well-known quote, "When the going gets tough, the tough get going." Absolutely true, as these are the very times, we tend to discover reservoirs of strength we never knew we possessed and use the opportunity to show what we are made of. Everything we can take on, succeed in overcoming, and move forward from, all builds on the knowledge and experience we may need for our next challenge. So, the next time you are battling through a tough situation, know that, in the end, it will make you even stronger than before, so you are getting something positive from it, even if you would rather not be experiencing it at all! Always a positive in the end!

November 25

"It doesn't matter what others are doing. It matters what YOU are doing." ~ *Unknown*

In our media culture it seems that everybody, especially the young and impressionable, are bombarded by the press and social media of what some "celebrity" is wearing, who is in a relationship with who, what their handbag or shoes cost, the list goes on and on. You know what I mean don't you? Of course, you do because you have the sense to realise that it is all fantasy, you will only be permitted to see what they want you to see, nothing more. Leave them to their shallow lives and focus on what YOU want to achieve in and from YOUR life. Always remember, YOU are important, YOU matter, and YOU impact on those around you. So, up to YOU now! YOUR choice!

November 26

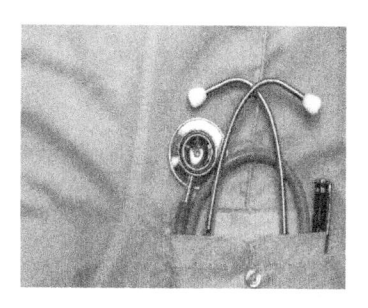

"Wisdom is nothing more than healed pain." ~ *Robert E. Lee*

Amen to that. This is the wisdom hard won by overcoming worrying times financially, dealing with a broken heart because of a failed relationship or the loss of a loved one, job, career, or business difficulties, etc. It helps us learn and absorb the lessons we are being taught, whether we realise it or not, in recognising the pain for what it is, a lesson in wisdom that we will keep with us for the future, and which will, no doubt, be added to in time. That is just life as we know it.

November 27

"Our life is what our thoughts make it."
~ Marcus Aurelias

Now there's a thought! If we imagine that our thoughts are the fuel that drives the engine that is our physical body, of course we would ensure we only put in the very best fuel we can. A fuel that is totally pure, without any impurities to "clog up the works" or impair its performance. It therefore follows that our "engine" would always be working to the best of its ability to take us to where we want or need to go. So, with life! Use your thought process to the best of your ability and see your life unfold as you wish it to be. Vroom, vroom!

November 28

"The World is changed by your example, not by your opinion." ~ *Paulo Coelho*

Of course, it is, we all know this don't we? That's why we all strive to be the best we can be in this troubled world of ours. Being the diverse human beings we are, naturally we all hold different opinions on everything and everyone. That's just the way it is. However, wouldn't it be absolutely amazing if the one thing we could ALL agree on was just to be the decent, tolerant, truthful, compassionate, people we are meant to be. Realising that being prepared to put our differences aside and work together will encourage others who follow us to do the same. What a wonderful world this could be, if only……

November 29

"The answers you seek never come when the mind is busy, they come when the mind is still." ~ *Leon Brown*

Busy, overactive, buzzing mind, with thoughts going round and round in a constant whirlpool of worry! How often has this happened to you? Many times? Yes, me too. However, I have found that just by sitting somewhere quietly and comfortably, I have been able to solely focus on stilling and quieting my mind. Occasionally, it can take more time than others but, eventually, my mind does become stiller and more peaceful, and it is then, and only then, that the answers I need take the opportunity to come forward. Try this the next time you find your head in a whirl of worry.

November 30

"Be the reason someone smiles today."
~ *Roy T. Bennett*

How wonderful to know that you are personally responsible for somebody smiling or laughing today. I know how much I appreciate it when my family or friends say or do something that makes me smile or laugh. I can totally relate to the saying that "laughter is the best medicine." The ability to instigate a smile or laughter is a very precious gift indeed, and one that we are all capable of giving at anytime, anywhere to anybody. So go, give...

December

368

December 1

"A diamond is a chunk of coal that did well under pressure." ~ *Henry Kissinger*

We are all diamonds! Each and every one of us. Shaped and moulded into the people we are and will become by how we cope and learn from the lesson's life teaches us. Just as it is necessary to use pressure to transform a lump of coal into something unique and precious, we also require pressure for our own transformation. There is nothing more unique or precious than every human being and their personal journey through transformation to completion...nothing.

December 2

"Your attitude determines your direction."
~ *Edwin Louis Cole*

I want you to picture your attitude as a steering wheel. Stay with me here...you have turned the key in the ignition and your "engine" is purring over nicely. You are ready to mirror, signal, maneuver but, hold on a moment, what's your destination? If you have no destination to aim for you are not going to get very far, are you? Even if you do drive off, you will be travelling aimlessly, fruitlessly, and needlessly. However, if you know exactly where you are heading for, then it is mirror, signal, maneuver, and away you go! Thank you, Attitude!

❀

December 3

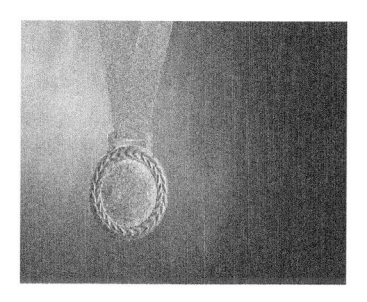

"Losers quit when they're tired. Winners quit when they've won." ~ *Mike Ditka*

That sums up very nicely the difference between what makes a loser and what makes a winner. There is no use aiming for success or achievement in something you have set your heart on if you are prepared to stumble, fall, and give up at the first hurdle is there? So now you know what you have to do. No matter how many hurdles, small, medium, or large, you must push yourself up and over, up, and over, repeatedly, if you want to be a winner not a loser. Not easy I know, but what is the alternative? Think about it.

December 4

shutterstock.com · 577461424

"Your best teacher is your last mistake."
~ Ralph Nader

Of course, it is, we all know that don't we? That is why it is essential to ensure that we do learn from each and every one of the mistakes we all make and will make as we journey through life. There is always a lesson to be gained. Hopefully, the lesson we need to learn will be an easy, straightforward, painless one. On the other hand, we may not be so fortunate and will find the learning process painful, frustrating, and difficult. However, there will always be something for us in the experience, you can count on it.

December 5

**"People inspire you, or they drain you –
pick wisely."** ~ *Hans F. Hansen*

Personally, I find it remarkably simple to pick wisely. I think we all sense quite quickly when we meet someone for the first time, whether he or she will be someone we want to get to know better. Occasionally, of course, as we are only human, our first impression may be misleading, and I realise this from past experience, and I expect you do too? That is just something to be expected. However, the process of being "picky" and deciding to exclude, (nicely of course), those people who do "drain" us can be instigated at any time in our relationship with them, so that is reassuring. Phew!

December 6

"Learn to appreciate what you have, before time makes you appreciate what you had."
~ *Unknown*

Unfortunately, for a great many of us, we do not realise what we do have until it is too late. Wishing we could turn back time in order to make amends and put things right is not an option. We are always going to carry the regret(s) with us and indeed wishing "if only" or "what if...?" So, to prevent this ever happening to you, take steps to show you appreciate who and what you have in your life. There are few sadder words than, "if only" and "what if?"

December 7

"Guilt is to the Spirit what pain is to the Body." ~ *Unknown*

I know we can all relate to suffering physical pain at some time in our lives. Whether mild or severe it still has an impact on how we cope or do not cope with its effects. Fortunately, however, there are numerous remedies readily available we can apply to find relief. It is a pity the same cannot be said when we seek relief from the guilt which we may be allowing to affect our Spirit. I say "allowing" because, unlike pain which strikes due to a physical ailment, guilt is of our own making. We have the power to dismiss guilt, refuse it a foothold, and deflect it just by our own thoughts, so why on earth would we give it power over us by recognising it? Consign it to the great cosmic waste basket where it belongs, and your Spirit will flourish and prosper as it should with nothing to hinder it. Sounds like a good plan, doesn't it?

December 8

"Tough situations build strong people."
~ Roy T. Bennett

They certainly do! This reminds me of another well-known quote, "When the going gets tough, the tough get going." Absolutely true, as these are the very times, we tend to discover reservoirs of strength we never knew we possessed and use the opportunity to show what we're made of. Everything we can take on, succeed in overcoming, and move forward from, all builds on the knowledge and experience we may need for our next challenge. So, the next time you're battling through a tough situation, know that, in the end, it will make you even stronger than before, so you are getting something positive from it, even if you'd rather not be experiencing it at all! Always a positive in the end!

December 9

"Happiness is an inside job. Don't assign anyone else that much power over you."
~ Mandy Hale

Oh, how true is this? Surely it makes sense for us to do our utmost to make US happy? Definitely an "inside job" therefore much too precious and valuable for us to consider even fleetingly allowing another influence over. Our own personal happiness, and where we find it, is solely our remit in life nobody else's. Of course, other people can and will bring happiness into our lives, this goes without saying but, at the end of the day, we need to remember that happiness comes from within us ourselves, from what we experience, what we know brings us joy. Do not allow others to take this from you.

December 10

"Forget what hurt you in the past but never forget what it taught you."
~ Shannon L. Alder

There will always be people, events or experiences in life that will cause us pain, either physical or emotional, that's just life. However, when looking back from the safety of the future, don't you occasionally get that "lightbulb" moment when you suddenly realise that you learned a valuable lesson? Not only that, but a lesson that proved beneficial to you in the future. So, it would be to your advantage to remember this the next time life trips you up, and it will, you can count on it.

December 11

"Surround yourself with people who empower you to become better."
~ *Unknown*

Oh, I do, I do! Everybody I know, family, friends, and colleagues, all inspire me to become a better me, not only as a person but at what I do to earn a living. I imagine you feel just the same? Through time, we all tend to whittle out those who serve no meaningful purpose in our life, the "takers" rather than the "givers." What remains is the cream of the crop, those who support us 100%, one hundred percent of the time in whatever we attempt and who feel genuine pleasure in our triumphs and achievements or are first to commiserate and wish us better luck next time. I hope these are the kind of people who presently inhabit your life but, if not, why not?

December 12

"It's not what you look at that matters, it's what you see." ~ *Henry David Thoreau*

Makes you think, doesn't it? I suppose occasionally we do not actually "see" who or what we are looking at every time we look at someone or something. Don't we all tend to see what we want to see? However, I guess this is just a small reminder that we need to be aware and take time to really appreciate and understand what we are seeing, be it another human being or something else. SEE beyond what your eyes are showing you, engage your heart and mind too. You may be surprised.

December 13

"Respect yourself if you would have others respect you." ~ *Baltasar Gracian*

Now, this is something we should all pay attention to. By instilling and maintaining your own sense of self-respect, which is how the world perceives you, earns you mutual respect in return. You do not need to be a mastermind to realise this do you? Think positively and kindly about you! You know you possess many positive attributes so why not make everybody else aware of them too? Be true to who you know yourself to be, the rules you live by, how you respect other's views and beliefs. Believe me, those who are fortunate enough to interact with you will notice and give you the respect you so deserve.

December 14

"Depth of friendship does not depend on length of acquaintance."
~ *Rabindranath Tagore*

Have you ever met someone and formed an instant connection? I like to think of these as past life connections, a person we may have known long ago. I have a friend I met when we were five years old - over the decades, whether we talked once a month or once a year, the depth of the friendship has never waned. On that same note, I have a dear friend whom I've known for less than a year, but it feels as if we are long-lost sisters, and the connection between us was instant! When we meet a kindred spirit, a friendship can form almost immediately, in the most surprising of ways!

December 15

"We do not remember days, we remember moments." ~ *Cesare Pavese*

I can very easily relate to this, and I expect you can too? Coloured mental video snapshots of those moments in life that transport us to another time, another place. Occasionally triggered by an old photo, a scent, revisiting a certain place, bumping into a face from the past... Moments that can create a smile, or perhaps a tear or two. This is what life is made up of. Every single day creates moments, both happy and sad, some of which we may reminisce about one day in the future. All part of the wonderful collage we call life. Let us hope your memories create many more smiles than tears.

December 16

"Go after your dream no matter how unattainable others think it is." ~ *Unknown*

Naysayers...they're everywhere! If I think back on how many times people told me I couldn't do something, which to me was merely a challenge, my life would be completely different. If you have a dream, a desire, or a mission, follow your heart! Taking that leap of faith off the clifftop of uncertainty will either teach you to fly or teach you a lesson in endurance. Either way, you win!

December 17

Sometimes those who challenge you most…. teach you the best." ~ *Unknown*

I can honestly say that hand on heart, I have met some really challenging people through the years. I won't bore you with the details, as I expect you've all got your own stories you could share too but, suffice to say, they have taught me valuable lessons. I know I didn't think so then and it was only later, usually much later, that I realised that I came out of the experience better equipped to deal with future challenging people. So, thank you, all you people who have challenged me in the past, thank you all very much indeed!

December 18

"What great thing would you attempt if you knew you could not fail?"
~ Robert H. Schuller

Oh, this made me think! I am not sure to be honest. What about you? Write a best-seller, explore a far-flung mysterious island, learn to pole dance, etc? However, I do not think this is so much about attempting something you know you will not fail at, as nudging you towards the realisation that, just by the very act of trying, you have already tasted success! There is success in every failed attempt don't you think? With the very intent and purpose of aiming for success you have proved yourself successful in thinking, planning, and creating something to aim for. Even if it does not prove "successful" in the way you had hoped in the end, you will have learned valuable lessons and gained insight along the way. So, next time………

December 19

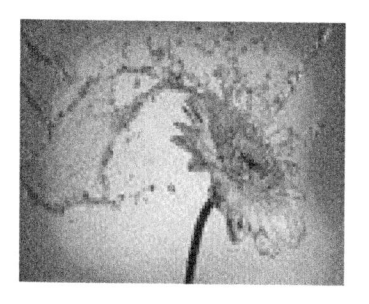

"Colours are the smiles of nature."
~ Leigh Hunt

So many colours for our eyes to feast on. Isn't nature wonderful? The changing of each season as it gradually morphs and unveils once again its unique, beautiful, inspirational, impressive, splendid palette of colour for our eyes to appreciate and marvel at. Man can never ever hope to compete with what Nature's very own specialist art gallery has to offer. From the delicate, intricate patterns to be found on butterflies, insects, animals, birds, plants, trees, etc., to the landscapes that take our breath away. Long may nature's art gallery always remain open for business. We are truly blessed.

December 20

"The secret of getting ahead is getting started." ~ *Mark Twain*

Very sensible advice if you ask me! We may have a great idea in mind, a task to perform, something we want to achieve, and so mentally work out how we are going to proceed. What materials (if any) will we require, tools, time scale, cost, etc. However, and this is vitally important, we need to take the physical steps or actions needed for us to progress or nothing will get done! In other words, put very simply, "Get your butt in gear and get going NOW!"

December 21

"Without hard work, nothing grows but weeds." ~ *Gordon B. Hinckley*

Let us imagine you have a garden, okay? Now, to keep this garden looking beautiful and a joy to behold, there is a great deal of effort and arduous work required. Constant care and attention, i.e., weeding, planting, watering, dead heading, and protection from predators and pests. Take a moment to compare this with your mind and/or life now. Can you see the similarity between the work needed to keep your physical garden in tip top condition and the work and attention needed, by you, to maintain, encourage and ensure your mind and life function to the absolute best of your ability? Happy gardening!

December 22

"Well done is better than well said."
~ *Benjamin Franklin*

A need to act rather than just talk about it is the clear meaning here. I guess a great many of us occasionally tend to tell all and sundry about a great plan, exciting enterprise, or original idea that we have had. Initially, everybody shares our enthusiasm, wishing us good luck and there may also be offers of financial or physical aid. However, after they have heard us talk about it, again, and again, and again, with nary a sign that we are taking steps to make it a reality, they all get fed up and leave. Wouldn't it be much better for them and us, if we did what we said, and earned a unanimous "Well done" rather than the consensus of" Here we go again!" Thought so.

December 23

**"Your life is your message to the World....
make it inspiring." ~ *Stuart Scott***

*Most of us are usually so busy just dealing with
our day-to-day lives that we never give a thought
to how others truly see us, or the impact our lives
may have on theirs. Stopping to think about how
we do want other people to perceive us may give
us pause to reflect on how we present ourselves.
We should be giving our all every day to be the
best and do the best we can as an example to all
those who look to us for guidance and support.
How great would that feel, to know that others
may gain inspiration and purpose just by our
example?*

December 24

"He that is discontented in one place, will seldom be happy in another." ~ *Aesop*

Discontentment is something felt within us, so attempting to just dismiss it, obviously will not work, will it? To get rid of this we must firstly understand why it is we are feeling discontented and, secondly, take steps in finding a resolution. Understand, there is absolutely nothing to be gained by physically upping sticks and moving, no matter the distance involved. Your discontent will just tag along with you. So, as we said, time to acknowledge your feelings and take whatever action you believe will give your discontent its marching orders. Hopefully, that's when discontent will find another home far, far away, and happiness can move in again.

December 25

"I will honour the Spirit of Christmas in my heart and keep it there all year."
~ *Unknown*

I love Christmas time, don't you? Everybody seems friendlier, more ready to say hello to a stranger, smiley faces evident everywhere, kindnesses being done and appreciated. Children (and me) buzzing with excitement and expectation. However, it's also the time when I wish that people all over the world could feel the Christmas Spirit all year round and not just for a short time every year. Wouldn't that be wonderful? As it's very unlikely that this will happen, it's up to each and every one of us to do our bit in using our own personal Christmas magic to make the world a better place each and every day, not just for a few special days every year.

December 26

"You must learn a new way to think before you can master a new way to be."
~ Marianne Williamson

Altering our mind-set to being more positive and, also more assertive, enables us to totally rethink who we are. Not only who we are at the present time, but who we aspire to be tomorrow, and the next day, and the next.... To even think of changing the way we approach and live life without taking time to firstly get our "think set" in gear, would prevent us from ever signalling and moving off. Know what I mean? Of course, you do!

December 27

"Our greatest battles are those with our own minds." ~ *Jameson Frank*

Okay, I confess, I cannot make a decision! Being asked to decide between two, or more options, puts me in total panic and I usually seek the opinion of those nearest to me. There is so much that goes on in our minds every day, not only while we are awake but also while we sleep. Continual battles rage in our heads daily. Having to make decisions, both minor and major, absorbing information, understanding it, dissecting it, and perhaps filing it away for future reference. This is the "hub" where everything is processed so there are bound to be times when our mind is a battleground, at odds with itself. However, we also possess the ability to bring the battle to an end to our own satisfaction if and when we choose, so all is not lost, is it?

December 28

"In life, surround yourself with those who light your path." ~ *Unknown*

I believe this to be the opposite of the saying "misery loves company. And it is so true that the nature of the people we surround ourselves with dictates our own nature. For example, family and friends whose very presence radiates love for us every time we are together and promotes a sense of peace and joy within us. Those who appreciate and accept us just as we are and who bring much into our lives just by being a part of our days. In return, allow yourself to be a loving light for them, one which burns brightly and resolutely.

December 29

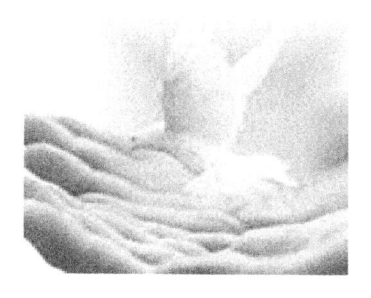

"It's not forgetting that heals, it's remembering." ~ *Amy Greene*

Sometimes our emotions become so overwhelming that we try to push them down, ignoring them in the hopes they will go away. And yet, any sadness or upset that we repress always finds a way to come back up. Allowing the feelings to move through us, remembering the positive aspects and gifts that are borne out of any loss or disappointment, gives all our life experience value. Acknowledging the past allows us to move beyond the pain so the healing process can begin.

December 30

"By being yourself, you put something wonderful in the world that wasn't there before." ~ *Edwin Elliot*

How much time do you suppose we spend comparing ourselves to others? I wish I had her hair, his money, their house... When we do this, our serenity and inner peace go right out the window! Instead of lamenting what you do not have, turn your perspective around by acknowledging the unique and wonderful presence you bring to the world. There truly is nobody else like you. Whatever we focus on grows stronger, so make it a point today to celebrate the real you!

December 31

"Years wrinkle the skin, but to give up enthusiasm wrinkles the soul."
~ *Dr. Frank Crane*

Never give your enthusiasm for anything or anyone the opportunity to slip away! Keep a tight grip on it whatever happens as it is one of your absolute best friends. It has served you well throughout your life and, just because you may be slathering on the anti-wrinkle cream at bedtime every night, does not mean your enthusiasm needs to lessen. Believe your enthusiasm is the anti-wrinkle cream for your soul, keep slathering it on and the results will continue to amaze you no matter how many wrinkles you have! The guarantee is on the box.

400

About the Author

Born in beautiful Paisley, Scotland, a long time ago…Married to Pete, she has two wonderful children Peter and Lianne, and two adored grandchildren, Oliver and Sienna. Catherine lives at the seaside in Kent, England.

Her Gran was a Medium and Tasseographer, so she grew up very aware and accepting of Spirit. Gifted with clairvoyance and a passion for tarot she has worked with both for many years, to provide insight, guidance and empowerment to all those she feels blessed to read for internationally and in the UK.

Catherine's inspirational and motivational quotes have been featured on www.kajama.com and she is also an Advice Columnist for "The Esotoracle" tarot publication.

Catherine's mantra, born from her passion for tarot, has always been, and always will be…

"I do what I love, and love what I do!"

Contact her at cathibewtarot@gmail.com

401

Printed in Great Britain
by Amazon

23349153R00225